"Finally a book that speaks to the wonderfully curious minds of children! *If I Could Ask God Anything* is a marvelous resource for parents and teachers to help start meaningful conversations with young kids about the heart of the Father and the journey of faith. I highly recommend it!"

The Rev. Ian Cron
Senior Minister, Trinity Church, Greenwich, Connecticut

"There are Sunday school teachers who know their Bible really well and there are Sunday school teachers who know kids really well. In Kathryn Slattery you'll meet a Sunday school teacher — and writer! — who knows her Bible <u>and</u> kids, and knows just how to bring the two together. What a resource for all of us Sunday school teachers with classrooms of kids!"

Rick Hamlin
Executive Editor, *Guideposts*

"I know this book will be an enormous help and encouragement to Christian parents looking for a friend to help them tackle some of their children's most challenging questions about God."

Dr. Hillary Bercovici
Scholar in Residence, Trinity Institute

"What my husband and I would have given to have this treasure of a book available when we were fumbling for answers to these very questions from <u>our</u> children!

Elizabeth Sherrill
Author of the best-selling inspirational classic, *The Hiding Place*

If I Could Ask God Anything

KATHRYN SLATTERY

THOMAS NELSON
Since 1798

NASHVILLE   DALLAS   MEXICO CITY   RIO DE JANEIRO   BEIJING

Cover Design: DeAnna Pierce, Bill Chiaravalle—Brand Navigation, LLC, www.brandnavigation.com
Cover Photo: Getty Images—Stockbyte Platinum
Interior: Kimberly Sagmiller—Visibility Creative, www.visibilitycreative.com

Library of Congress Cataloging-in-Publication Data
ISBN 13: 978-1-59145-411-3

Printed in the United States of America
08 09 RRD 9 8 7 6 5 4 3

Contents

The Church

Christian Seasons and Holidays

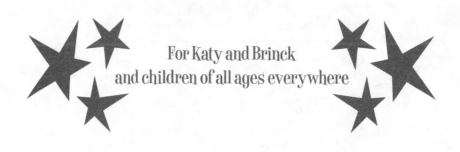

For Katy and Brinck
and children of all ages everywhere

Acknowledgments

With special gratitude and love to all the children
of Trinity Church, Greenwich, Connecticut and
St. Mark's Episcopal Church, New Canaan, Connecticut.
Thank you for your inquisitive minds, your great
big hearts, and the many excellent questions
you contributed to this book.

Note to Parents

Children, like grown-ups, need faith. We are now living in what historians and many theologians call the "post-Christian" age. Secular humanism, moral relativism, materialism, and political correctness have created a moral atmosphere of murky gray where there are few absolutes to help parents and children discern right from wrong. Even the way we do something as fundamental as note the passage of time has been secularly redefined. In academic circles, BC, which traditionally stands for "before Christ," has been replaced by the more politically correct BCE, or "before the common era." Likewise, AD, which stands for the Latin *anno Domini*, or, "in the year of our Lord," has been replaced by CE, or "of the common era."

Today, more than ever, children need to be informed and reassured that God is real, that He personally loves them, and that He has a unique purpose for each of their lives. What the late, great Christian apologist C. S. Lewis called "mere Christianity" can make a powerful, positive difference in a child's life. Young people can be motivated and empowered by faith to make a positive difference in a fallen and hurting world. Children can and should be able to articulate what they believe and why they believe it.

We can rejoice that children enter this world with a tremendous capacity for faith. For children, believing in God is instinctive. It is as natural as breathing. As Jesus said, "Let the little children come to me, and do not hinder them, for the kingdom of God belongs to such as these" (Mark 10:14; Luke 18:16).

It is not only our privilege but also our responsibility to nurture our children's God-given faith. Typically, our children's Christian education includes involvement in Sunday school, familiarity with the Bible, and routine prayers at meals and bedtimes. But that's not really enough. It takes a personal, intimate relationship with a loving God to breathe life and meaning into these religious traditions. As a Sunday school teacher, I have been stunned to discover how little my students know about the basics of the Christian faith, let alone about the Bible and the church.

If I Could Ask God Anything offers clear, fresh answers in language that kids can understand to a wide variety of questions that ultimately cover the basic tenets of biblically based orthodox Christianity, such as:

If God is invisible, how can I know He is real?

Why did Jesus have to die?

How can God be three persons at the same time?

How can I know for sure that Jesus really was resurrected?

What is communion?

It also includes answers to fun and challenging questions such as:

Does God ever sleep?

Did Jesus live on earth before or after the dinosaurs?

When I die, will I become an angel with a halo and wings?

Are Saint Nicholas and Santa Claus the same person?

Is it OK to pray for help on a test?

If I Could Ask God Anything will deepen young readers' understanding of how faith works in their own lives, and help them see how they fit into the larger body of Christ at work in the world today. Most importantly, this book is written with the aim of helping young readers establish a deep and lasting personal relationship with a living, loving God through faith in Jesus Christ.

If I Could Ask God Anything is, quite frankly, the book I wish my two children had when they were young. It is also the book I wish I had during my many years teaching Sunday school.

I encourage you to explore the questions in this book with your child and grow in faith together. And don't be surprised when your child teaches you!

There are, of course, an infinite number of questions about God—more than could ever be answered in one book. When your child comes to you with difficult questions, you may find that your own faith is challenged. When there seems to be no satisfactory answer for a question, don't be afraid to say, "I don't know" or, "Let's look in the Bible" or, "Let's ask our pastor about that."

In the end, you and your child will gain a clearer understanding of exactly what you believe and why. Remember, God loves a seeking heart (Matthew 7:7–12)

And God loves *you*.

—Kathryn Slattery

New Canaan, Connecticut

Visit the author at www.KathrynSlattery.com

Who Is God?

God is the creator of everything, visible and invisible. God created heaven and the angels. God created time and space. From God's fingertips tumbled galaxies, stars, the sun, the moon, and our beautiful planet earth. God loved His creation so much that He didn't stop there. God created the oceans, the animals, the birds in the sky, and the fish in the sea. God created human beings (Genesis 1–2).

God created *you*!

Every child has a biological or earthly mother and father. Earthly moms and dads are not perfect. Because they are human, they make mistakes. Earthly moms and dads can get tired and grumpy. They can have problems and get divorced. Because they are human, earthly parents can get hurt or sick and die.

The good news is that every child also has a spiritual parent, known as our Father God in heaven. God loves us perfectly and never gets tired or grumpy or sick. Best of all, God never dies.

God's children include all the people on earth. God's children include people who are living and people who have died. Do you know someone who is expecting a baby? God's children even include people who haven't been born yet (Psalm 139:13–16).

Here's the best news: You are a child of God!

(1 John 3:1)

? Who is God?
➤ God is your **Creator** and your **perfect Parent.**

? What is the best word to describe what God is like?
➤ **God is love.** (1 John 4:8)

Where Did God Come From?

The Bible says that God is both the beginning and the end (Revelation 21:6). This is because God is eternal. The word *eternal* means endless. How can God be eternal?

God is uncreated. God is not limited by time and space. God existed before the dawn of time. God created time!

God is unchanging. He is the same today as He was yesterday. He will be the same tomorrow. This is a hard idea for our human minds to understand. But it is true. You can always count on God.

 The Bible says,

"Give thanks to the LORD, for he is good. His love endures forever"
(Psalm 136:1).

Because God is eternal, so is His love for you.

If God Is Invisible, How Can I Know He Is Real?

There are many things we can't see with our eyes, yet we know they are real. For example, we can't see gravity, but we know it is real. How do we know gravity is real? Because if you let go of this book, it will drop to the floor with a big thud!

Are you sitting in a room that is cooled by an electric fan or air conditioner? Is the page you are reading lit by an electric light? We can't see electricity, but we know it is real.

And what about your thoughts? Until you speak them out loud or write them on a piece of paper, your thoughts are invisible. Still, they are very real.

My favorite example of how we can know God is real even though we can't see Him is the wind (John 3:8). We can't see the wind, but we know it is real because we can feel it when it cools our skin on a hot summer day. We can't see the wind, but we can see treetops swaying. We can see clouds racing across the sky. We can see whitecaps on a choppy ocean. Sometimes the wind is a gentle breeze that barely stirs the leaves on the trees. Other times it blows as a mighty hurricane or tornado. We can also hear the wind when it whistles, whispers, moans, and roars.

God is like the wind.

Listen to what God is saying:

I am real. I created you. I love you.
There is no other human being quite like you. You are special.
I created you for Myself, and I have a very special purpose
for your life on planet earth.

More than anything, God wants you to know that He is real and that He loves you (1 John 3:1).

How Can I Know for Sure God Loves Me?

God is busy, that's for sure. He sends us sunshine by day and moonlight by night. He sends the snow and rain. He sends us flowers in the spring and beautiful colored leaves in the fall. God keeps the planets in their orbits and the stars in the sky. Because God does so much, it would be easy to think that He is too busy to love His billions of children.

But God is not like us. God is perfect. With His perfect memory, He knows each and every person's name. Imagine that!

God knows *your* name. God loves and cares for you a *lot*.

The Bible says that God cares so much about His creation that He knows every time a sparrow falls from the sky (Matthew 10:29). He knew you even before you were born (Psalm 139:13–16). God even knows exactly how many hairs are on your head! (Matthew 10:30). God loves you *so* much that He watches over you every minute of every day and night—even right now, as you are reading these words (Psalm 139:1–10).

There is another way you can know God loves you. Sometimes God speaks to you in your heart. Sometimes He calls you by your name. Although God is big and strong, His voice is a gentle whisper (1 Kings 19:12). Close your eyes and listen.

Can you hear God's voice calling your name?

Can you hear God's voice whispering *I love you*?

Even when you can't hear God's voice, He loves you. Because God is your perfect Father in heaven, He always loves you with His perfect love (1 John 3:1).

? How do you know God loves you?

➡ Because the **Bible** tells you so.

18

Who Is the Trinity?

Over the years, this three-Person understanding of God became known as the Trinity. The word *trinity* means three in one. The Trinity is a way to describe God.

The Bible teaches that God is made up of **three** persons:

(Matthew 28:19)

1. God
2. God's Son, Jesus
3. God's Holy Spirit

How Can God Be Three Persons at the Same Time?

There are many examples to help us understand how God can be three different Persons at the same time. Take an egg, for example. An egg consists of three parts: the shell, the white, and the yolk. But the shell, the white, and the yolk are all part of the same egg. Or think about the relationships that you have with three different people in your life. You may be a daughter to your parents, a sister to your brother, and a niece to your aunt and uncle. But at the same time, you are still you.

Another great example of how God can be three Persons at the same time is water. When water is room temperature, it is a flowing liquid. When water is heated up in a teakettle, it becomes steam. When water is frozen, it becomes ice. But it is always water. The different forms that water takes enable it to serve different purposes.

God, your Father in heaven, is watching over you and waiting for you to join Him one day. God's Son, Jesus, walked and talked on earth to show people who God really is and to die for your sins. Jesus is in heaven now, sitting next to His Father. God's Holy Spirit is not limited by time or space, which allows God to live in your heart. The Holy Spirit guides you and whispers God's love to you.

The reason God is three Persons in one is so He can be with you every minute of every day.

? Why does God want to be with you every minute of every day?
➤ Because **God loves you.**
(John 3:1)

How Do I Know God Has a Special Purpose for My Life?

When God makes snowflakes, each one is different. Some are big. Some are tiny. Some are star-shaped and pointy. Some are lacy and round. Some are heavy and wet. Some are light and fluffy.

If God makes billions and billions of different snowflakes, think how different and special He makes each one of His children!

You are special. There is no one else on earth exactly like you. Even if you are an identical twin, you are different and special on the inside. You are special because God has special work for you to do during your life. It is work that *only you* can do. It is the reason you were born.

You can know God has a special purpose for your life because the Bible says He knew you and loved you even before you were born (Psalm 139:13–16). You are God's special child, created to do good works (Ephesians 2:10). No one else can do these kind and helpful acts. God has prepared them for you—and only you—to do. Your mission in life is to discover what these good works are. Talk about an exciting adventure!

Here is a hint: the good works God has planned for you to do always have to do with *love*. You can be sure you are discovering God's special purpose for your life when you:

Tell your mom and dad you love them.
Hug your grandma and grandpa.
Write your favorite aunt a letter and tell her how much you love and miss her.
Thank your teacher for working so hard.
Invite the new kid in school to sit with you at lunch.
Tell your friend you're sorry you hurt her feelings.
Listen to your friend who is sad.
Pray for your friend who is sick.
Show love for others by helping.
Show God how much you love Him by trying to love others.

What Does It Mean That I'm Created "In the Image of God"?

The Bible says that human beings are created "in the image of God" (Genesis 1:27).

Because you are God's child, you are like God in many ways. Because God is loving, you can be loving. Because God has a sense of humor, you can laugh. Because God is joyful, you can be joyful. Because God knows sadness, you can cry. Because God is eternal, you have a soul that is eternal. Because God knows and loves you, it is possible for you to know and love Him (1 John 4:19).

God loves you so much that He wants you to live with Him forever!

God loves you so much, in fact, that the Bible says that nothing—not even sickness or death—can separate you from His love (Romans 8:38–39).

How Can I Get to Know God Better?

When it comes to knowing God, kids are natural-born experts. It is grown-ups who often forget how to believe in God and that they need extra help! Jesus said, "Let the little children come to me, and do not hinder them, for the kingdom of God belongs to such as these" (Mark 10:14; Luke 18:16). Then Jesus probably smiled as He gathered up the children in His arms and hugged them.

Here are three good ways to get to know God better:

1. Read your Bible. The Bible is God's love letter to you. The more you read the Bible, the more you will get to know and love God.

2. Spend time with God in prayer. Prayer is talking and listening to God. The best way to get to know someone is to spend time with that person. Spend time with God, and you will get to know Him better. God is waiting to hear from you! When you pray, God listens carefully. God speaks to you in your heart, and answers your prayers with His gentle voice (1 Kings 19:12; Psalm 34:15—17; 1 Peter 3:12). Sometimes God's answers are not what you might expect. Sometimes He says no or wait. But because God loves you, you can trust that He knows what is best for you.

3. Spend time with friends who believe in God. Friends who believe in God can share with one another what they know about God. Friends who believe in God can pray with and for one another. You will be amazed how much *fun* it is to be friends with kids who believe in God!

Do you know what God thinks about you wanting to get to know Him better? It makes Him *so-o-o-o-o-o-o* happy! Why does it make God happy? Because *God loves you* (1 John 3:1).

When God Looks at Me, What Does He See?

When God looks at you, He sees what other people see. He sees the outside. He sees the color of your hair and eyes. He sees you sitting at your desk in school. He sees you doing your homework. He sees you riding your bike. He sees you eating dinner. He sees you watching TV. He sees you talking on the phone with your friend. He even sees you when you are sleeping. God loves all these things about you.

But God also sees something else.

When God looks at you, He sees the *inside* of you too (1 Samuel 16:7; 1 Chronicles 28:9). In fact, God is more interested in who you are on the inside than who you are on the outside. This is because who you are on the inside lasts forever and ever.

Who you are on the inside is called your soul. Your soul is made up of all your thoughts, feelings, dreams, and desires. Your soul is made up of the love in your heart. Are you kind to others? Are you honest? Do you like to laugh? These are the things that are important to God. These are who you really are. Even when your body dies, your soul lives on forever.

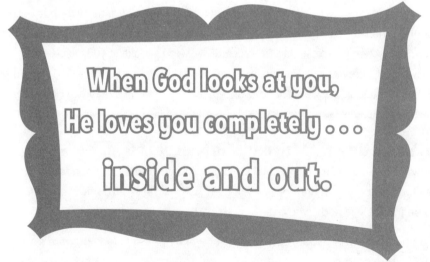

When God looks at you,
He loves you completely . . .
inside and out.

God loves you so much that He wants you to live forever and ever with Him in heaven (John 3:16)!

Does God Care Whether My Body Is Skinny or Fat?

God does not care whether your body is skinny or fat. God does not care whether you are short or tall. God does not care whether your skin is brown or beige. God creates His children in all shapes, sizes, and colors. God loves *all* His children.

The Bible tells us that God made each of us "in an amazing and wonderful way" (Psalm 139:14 NCV). Because God made you special, you are one of a kind. Think about it. No one else has a body quite like yours! No matter what your body looks like or how it works, God loves you just the way you are.

At the same time, God wants your body to be as healthy as possible. He wants your soul to be healthy too (1 Thessalonians 5:23; 3 John 2).

Here are some ways to have a healthy body:

Eat foods that are good for you.

Get lots of sunshine and as much exercise as you can.

Get enough sleep.

Here are some ways to have a healthy soul:

Talk and listen to God in prayer.

Read your Bible.

Spend time with friends who love God too.

Read books and watch TV shows that are wholesome and fun.

? Why does God want you to have a healthy body and soul?

➡ Because **God loves you.**

(1 John 3:1)

What Do I Have to Do to Get God to Love Me?

Here is good news: You don't have to do anything to get God to love you! God loves you just the way you are (1 John 3:1). God loves you because you are His child. It's as simple as that.

God Loves You!

Does God Ever Sleep?

Because God loves you, He is always watching out for you. Because God is not human, He never gets tired or needs to sleep.

The Bible says, "The eyes of the Lord search back and forth across the whole earth, looking for people whose hearts are perfect toward him, so that he can show his great power in helping them" (2 Chronicles 16:9 TLB). The Bible says, "The LORD sees the good people and listens to their prayers" (Psalm 34:15 NCV). The Bible also says that nothing, not even death, can separate us from God's watchful eye and His love! (Psalm 139:1–18; Romans 8:38–39).

At the same time, God understands how important it is for us to rest—especially after working hard. The Bible tells us that God worked for six days on His creation. He created the sun, the moon, the stars, and earth. He created all the birds in the sky, the fish in the sea, and all the animals. He created the first humans, Adam and Eve. And what did God do after all that creating? The Bible says that on the seventh day, God rested (Genesis 2:1–3).

The idea of taking time to rest is so important that God made a commandment about it: "Remember the Sabbath day by keeping it holy" (Exodus 20:8). The word *sabbath* means to rest. Resting is good for our bodies. It is also good for our souls.

When you rest, there is only one thing that God wants you to do.

> # God wants you to remember
> ## that He loves you.
> (1 John 3:1)

What Are Some of God's Promises for Me?

Do you ever feel down in the dumps? Lonely? Worried? Guilty? Confused? Jealous? Angry? Everyone feels bad sometimes. It's part of being human. Because God cares about you, He knows when you are feeling low. Because God loves you, He wants to help you feel better (1 Peter 5:7). One way God helps you is through the Bible.

Remember, the Bible is not a dry, boring book. It is the living Word of God! Through the Bible, God is able to speak to you personally. In fact, the Bible is full of God's promises just for you. This is good news! Why? Because God always keeps His promises (Deuteronomy 7:9; 1 Corinthians 1:9).

Here are a few of God's promises for you!

When you are lonely . . .

▶ "I am with you and will watch over you wherever you go" (Genesis 28:15).

▶ "I will not leave you . . . I will come to you" (John 14:18).

▶ "Surely I am with you always, to the very end of the age" (Matthew 28:20).

▶ "Who shall separate us from the love of Christ? Shall trouble or hardship or persecution or famine or nakedness or danger or sword? . . . No, in all these things we are more than conquerors through him who loved us. For I am convinced that neither death nor life, neither angels nor demons, neither the present nor the future, nor any powers, neither height nor depth, nor anything else in all creation, will be able to separate us from the love of God that is in Christ Jesus our Lord" (Romans 8:35, 37–39).

When you are sad...

➧ "The Lord is close to the brokenhearted and saves those who are crushed in spirit" (Psalm 34:18).

➧ "Then they cried to the Lord in their trouble, and he saved them from their distress" (Psalm 107:19).

➧ "I have told you these things, so that in me you may have peace. In this world you will have trouble. But take heart! I have overcome the world" (John 16:33).

➧ "And God's peace, which is so great we cannot understand it, will keep your hearts and minds in Christ Jesus" (Philippians 4:7 NCV).

When you are worried...

➧ "Give all your worries to [God], because he cares about you" (1 Peter 5:7 NCV).

➧ "Give your worries to the LORD, and he will take care of you" (Psalm 55:22 NCV).

➧ "Do not let your hearts be troubled. Trust in God; trust also in me" (John 14:1).

➧ "Come to me, all you who are weary and burdened, and I will give you rest" (Matthew 11:28).

➧ "Peace I leave with you; my peace I give you. . . . Do not let your hearts be troubled and do not be afraid" (John 14:27).

➧ "Do not worry about your life, what you will eat or drink; or about your body, what you will wear. . . . Look at the birds of the air; they do not sow or reap or store away in barns, and yet your heavenly Father feeds them. Are you not much more valuable than they? Who of you by worrying can add a single hour to his life. . . . So do not worry" (Mathew 6:25–27, 31).

When you are **afraid...**

➡ "So don't worry, because I am with you. Don't be afraid, because I am your God. I will make you strong and will help you; I will support you with my right hand that saves you" (Isaiah 41:10 NCV).

➡ "The LORD is my light and my salvation—whom shall I fear? The LORD is the stronghold of my life—of whom shall I be afraid?" (Psalm 27:1).

➡ "Be strong and courageous. Do not be terrified; do not be discouraged, for the LORD your God will be with you wherever you go" (Joshua 1:9).

➡ "God did not give us a spirit that makes us afraid but a spirit of power and love and self-control" (2 Timothy 1:7 NCV).

➡ "God is our refuge and strength, an ever-present help in trouble. Therefore we will not fear" (Psalm 46:1–2).

When you are **jealous...**

➡ "Be content with what you have, because God has said, 'Never will I leave you; never will I forsake you'" (Hebrews 13:5).

➡ "Seek first his kingdom and his righteousness, and all these things will be given to you as well" (Matthew 6:33).

➡ "No eye has seen, no ear has heard, no mind has conceived what God has prepared for those who love him" (1 Corinthians 2:9).

When you are **angry...**

➡ "'In your anger do not sin': Do not let the sun go down while you are still angry" (Ephesians 4:26).

➡ "Everyone should be quick to listen, slow to speak and slow to become angry, for man's anger does not bring about the righteous life that God desires" (James 1:19–20).

➡ "Don't get angry. Don't be upset; it only leads to trouble" (Psalm 37:8 NCV).

➡ "A gentle answer turns away wrath, but a harsh word stirs up anger" (Proverbs 15:1).

When you are confused and need guidance...

➡ "The LORD will guide you always; he will satisfy your needs" (Isaiah 58:11).

➡ "For this God is our God for ever and ever; he will be our guide even to the end" (Psalm 48:14).

➡ "Whether you turn to the right or to the left, your ears will hear a voice behind you, saying, 'This is the way; walk in it'" (Isaiah 30:21).

➡ "I will instruct you and teach you in the way you should go; I will counsel you and watch over you" (Psalm 32:8).

➡ "If any of you lacks wisdom, he should ask God, who gives generously to all without finding fault, and it will be given to him. But when he asks, he must believe and not doubt" (James 1:5–6).

➡ "Ask and it will be given to you; seek and you will find; knock and the door will be opened to you. For everyone who asks receives; he who seeks finds; and to him who knocks, the door will be opened" (Matthew 7:7–8).

When you are sick...

➡ "I will restore you to health and heal your wounds" (Jeremiah 30:17).

➡ "The LORD will sustain him on his sickbed and restore him from his bed of illness" (Psalm 41:3).

➡ "I will bind up the injured and strengthen the weak" (Ezekiel 34:16).

➡ "He gives strength to the weary and increases the power of the weak. Even youths grow tired and weary, and young men stumble and fall; but those who hope in the LORD will renew their strength. They will soar on wings like eagles; they will run and not grow weary, they will walk and not be faint" (Isaiah 40:29–31).

➡ "The prayer offered in faith will make the sick person well; the Lord will raise him up" (James 5:15).

When you need more faith...

➡ "Faith comes from hearing the message, and the message is heard through the word of Christ" (Romans 10:17).

➡ "We live by what we believe, not by what we can see" (2 Corinthians 5:7 NCV).

➡ "What is impossible with men is possible with God" (Luke 18:27).

➡ "I tell you the truth, if you have faith as small as a mustard seed, you can say to this mountain, 'Move from here to there' and it will move. Nothing will be impossible for you" (Matthew 17:20).

➡ "Everything is possible for him who believes" (Mark 9:23).

When you are tempted...

➡ "No temptation has seized you except what is common to man. And God is faithful; he will not let you be tempted beyond what you can bear. But when you are tempted, he will also provide a way out so that you can stand up under it" (1 Corinthians 10:13).

➡ "Because he himself suffered when he was tempted, he is able to help those who are being tempted" (Hebrews 2:18).

➡ "Consider it pure joy, my brothers, whenever you face trials of many kinds, because you know that the testing of your faith develops perseverance" (James 1:2–3).

When you feel guilty...

➡ "If we confess our sins, he is faithful and just, and will forgive our sins and cleanse us from all unrighteousness" (1 John 1:9 RSV).

➡ "So now, those who are in Christ Jesus are not judged guilty" (Romans 8:1 NCV).

➡ "For I will forgive their wickedness and will remember their sins no more" (Jeremiah 31:34).

➡ "For sin shall not be your master, because you are not under law, but under grace" (Romans 6:14).

➡ "Everyone who calls on the name of the Lord will be saved" (Acts 2:21).

➡ "Let us come near to God with a sincere heart and a sure faith, because we have been made free from a guilty conscience" (Hebrews 10:22 NCV).

When you have failed...

➡ "The LORD upholds all those who fall and lifts up all who are bowed down" (Psalm 145:14).

➡ "Whoever trusts in the LORD is kept safe" (Proverbs 29:25).

➡ "For though a righteous man falls seven times, he rises again" (Proverbs 24:16).

➡ "We are hard pressed on every side, but not crushed; perplexed, but not in despair; persecuted, but not abandoned; struck down, but not destroyed" (2 Corinthians 4:8–9).

When you need hope...

➡️ "Be strong and take heart, all you who hope in the Lord" (Psalm 31:24).

➡️ "'For I know the plans I have for you,' declares the Lord, 'plans to prosper you and not to harm you, plans to give you hope and a future'" (Jeremiah 29:11).

➡️ "We also rejoice in our sufferings, because we know that suffering produces perseverance; perseverance, character; and character, hope. And hope does not disappoint us, because God has poured out his love into our hearts by the Holy Spirit, whom he has given us" (Romans 5:3–5).

➡️ "And we know that in all things God works for the good of those who love him, who have been called according to his purpose" (Romans 8:28).

When you feel left out by others...

➡️ "He heals the brokenhearted and binds up their wounds" (Psalm 147:3).

➡️ "Never will I leave you; never will I forsake you" (Hebrews 13:5).

➡️ "The Lord loves justice and will not leave those who worship him" (Psalm 37:28 NCV).

➡️ "If God is for us, who can be against us?" (Romans 8:31).

➡️ "And even the very hairs of your head are all numbered. So don't be afraid; you are worth more than many sparrows" (Matthew 10:30–31).

When someone you love has **died...**

➡ "God will wipe away every tear from their eyes" (Revelation 7:17).

➡ "The LORD comforts his people and will have compassion on his afflicted ones" (Isaiah 49:13).

➡ "The LORD is good to all; he has compassion on all he has made" (Psalm 145:9).

➡ "There will be no more death or mourning or crying or pain, for the old order of things has passed away. He who was seated on the throne said, 'I am making everything new!'" (Revelation 21:4–5).

Who Is Jesus?

Jesus is God's only Son (Mark 14:61–62). Jesus is the most important person who ever lived in the history of our world.

In his Gospel, John wrote that Jesus Is:

➡ the Word (John 1:14)

➡ the Lamb of God (John 1:29, 36)

➡ the Messiah (John 1:41)

➡ the Son of God (John 1:49)

➡ the King of Israel (John 1:49)

➡ the Savior of the world (John 4:42)

➡ the Lord and God (John 20:28)

When Was Jesus Born?

Jesus was born a little over two thousand years ago in the tiny town of Bethlehem, in the country of Israel. We know this is true. It is not a myth, legend, or fairy tale. It is an honest-to-goodness historical fact (Luke 2:1–7).

But because Jesus was born so many years ago, before there were things like personal computers and the Internet, we don't know for sure exactly what year Jesus was born. Many scholars put the date at about 4–5 BC. We also don't know the exact address. Scholars believe that Jesus was probably born in a stable, which is like a small barn. This is because the Bible says that after Jesus was born, His mother Mary placed the baby Jesus in a *manger*, or wooden feeding box for animals (Luke 2:16).

Why Was Jesus Born in a Stable?

At the time of Jesus' birth, the Roman world was ruled by a king named Caesar Augustus. Augustus ordered that all the people be registered in a world-wide census (Luke 2:1). Jesus' mother Mary and her fiancé Joseph were from a town in Israel called Nazareth. They traveled to Bethlehem to be counted in the census.

When Mary and Joseph arrived in Bethlehem, the town was very crowded. Even though Mary was expecting a baby, there was no room at the village inn. Hospitals hadn't been invented yet. So Mary and Joseph had to stay in a stable.

When Jesus was born, Mary wrapped Him in *swaddling clothes* or strips of cloth to keep Him snug and warm. Then she gently placed the baby Jesus in a manger (Luke 2:7).

How Did Jesus Get His Name?

Months before Mary even knew she was going to have a baby; an angel visited her and Joseph. As you can imagine, they were both very surprised!

"You are going to have a son," the angel Gabriel announced to Mary. "And His true Father will be God in heaven." The angel told Mary and Joseph to name the baby boy Jesus, which means "Savior" or "one who saves the people."

> Because Mary and Joseph **loved** and **trusted** God, they did what Gabriel said and named the boy **Jesus.**
>
> (Matthew 1:25; Luke 1:26–38; 2:21)

What Is the Song of Mary?

Mary was a very young woman when the angel Gabriel visited her. She loved God with all her heart, soul, and mind. When Gabriel told Mary that God had picked her to have His Son, Mary could hardly believe her ears. She wasn't even married yet!

On top of everything, Gabriel also told Mary that her cousin Elizabeth was six months pregnant. *How could this be?* Mary thought. Elizabeth was very old and unable to have children.

"Nothing is impossible with God," said Gabriel (Luke 1:37).

Mary loved her cousin Elizabeth. She quickly traveled to Judah, the town where Elizabeth lived. When Elizabeth heard the sound of Mary's voice, her unborn baby jumped in her womb. She was filled with God's Holy Spirit.

"Blessed are you among women," Elizabeth said to Mary. "And blessed is the child you will bear!" (Luke 1:42). Mary remembered what the angel Gabriel had told her. She, too, was filled with the Holy Spirit. She felt so humbled and honored. She thought her heart would burst for joy.

Mary's beautiful response to Elizabeth is known as the Song of Mary. It is also called the *Magnificat*, from a Latin word that means to magnify. This is because in some versions of the Bible the first words Mary says are, "My soul doth magnify the Lord" (Luke 1:46 KJV).

Here is the song of Mary from the New Century Version of the Bible:

My soul praises the Lord;

my heart rejoices in God my Savior,

because he has shown his concern for his humble servant girl.

From now on, all people will say that I am blessed,

because the Powerful One has done great things for me.

His name is holy.

God will show his mercy forever and ever

to those who worship and serve him.

He has done mighty deeds by his power.

He has scattered the people who are proud

and think great things about themselves.

He has brought down rulers from their thrones

and raised up the humble.

He has filled the hungry with good things

and sent the rich away with nothing.

He has helped his servant, the people Israel,

remembering to show them mercy

as he promised to our ancestors,

to Abraham and to his children forever.

(Luke 1:46–55)

What Was Jesus Like When He Was a Boy?

The Bible tells us that Jesus was a strong, active, healthy boy (Luke 2:40). Mary and her husband, Joseph, were good parents, and they raised their son to be obedient and to love God.

Jesus was also very smart and brave. When Jesus was twelve years old, He was separated from His parents while visiting the big city of Jerusalem. Three days later, Mary and Joseph found Jesus in the temple courtyard. He was sitting among the grown-up teachers, listening to them and talking to them about the Scriptures.

"Everyone who heard [Jesus] was amazed at his understanding and his answers" (Luke 2:47). Jesus was calm as can be. Not worried at all. But His mother was very upset.

"Son, why have you treated us like this?" Mary asked. "Your father and I have been anxiously searching for you" (Luke 2:48).

"Why were you searching for me?" Jesus asked. "Didn't you know I had to be in my Father's house?" (Luke 2:49).

Mary and Joseph didn't understand that when Jesus said, "I had to be in my Father's house," He was talking about His Father God, in heaven.

Did Jesus Ever Do Anything Wrong?

We know from the Bible that Jesus was tempted like any other human being (Matthew 4:1–11; Mark 1:12–13; Luke 4:1–13). But because Jesus is God's Son, He never gave in to temptation (Hebrews 4:15). He never did anything wrong. Not once!

Jesus was fully human. At the same time, Jesus said, "Anyone who has seen me has seen the Father" (John 14:9). By this, Jesus meant that He and God are one and the same.

When Jesus was tempted to do wrong, He prayed and asked God to help Him. Jesus loved and trusted God, and God answered His prayers. Because Jesus suffered when He was tempted, He is able to help us when we are tempted too (Hebrews 2:18).

Because Jesus was perfect, He didn't live for money or fame.

All Jesus wanted during His life on earth was to do His Father's will. All Jesus wanted was to show the world how much God loves us.

This is what Jesus wants us to try to do too!

Is Jesus' Last Name Christ?

The word *Christ* comes from a Greek word that means messiah or anointed one. "Christ" is more accurately a title than a name.

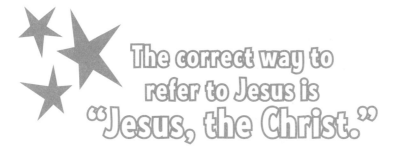

The correct way to refer to Jesus is "Jesus, the Christ."

But over the years, people have tended to run His name and title together.

In the Old Testament, God promised that He would one day send a messiah to save His people and be their King forever and ever (Psalms 2; 16:10; 22; 23; 110; Isaiah 4:2; 7:14; 11; 40:11; 53; 61:1–3). Jesus is that person (John 1:41).

What Makes Jesus So Important?

Jesus is not just any human being. Jesus is the most important person who ever lived in the history of our world. Jesus said that He was God's very own Son (Mark 14:61–62). No one had ever said that before!

Jesus was so close to God that when He prayed, or talked to God, He used the word *"Abba"* (Mark 14:36). In Jesus' native Aramaic language, the word *abba* means daddy or papa. Imagine that!

Jesus was so close to God that He said, "I and the Father are one" (John 10:30). Jesus also said, "Anyone who has seen me has seen the Father" (John 14:9).

Jesus is different from all other religious leaders who ever lived in the history of the world because He was raised from the dead.

Jesus is alive today with His Father in heaven. He is alive in our hearts through God's Holy Spirit.

Because Jesus is alive, He knows and loves you. Because Jesus is alive, you can know and love Him.

This is very good news!

Why Did Jesus Come to Earth?

Jesus said that God, His Father in heaven, sent Him to earth to bring people a full and wonderful life (John 10:10). Jesus said that God sent Him to show people everywhere once and for all what God is really like (John 14:6–7). Jesus said that God sent Him to forgive the sins of everyone who would believe in Him, so that they could live forever with God in heaven (Mark 16:15–16).

When Jesus was born, it was as though God Himself put skin on and came crashing into human history!

Until Jesus was born, no one had ever really seen God. No one was sure what God was really like. Was God friendly? Or was He grumpy? Was God happy? Or was He gloomy? Did God cry? Did God laugh? Did God even think or care about His children at all? Or was He too busy doing important things like keeping the stars up in the sky and the planets from bumping into each other?

Jesus said that God cares about each and every one of us . . . including you . . . a lot.

"For God so loved the world," said Jesus, "that he gave his one and only Son, that whoever believes in him shall not perish but have eternal life" (John 3:16).

Did Jesus Live on Earth Before or After the Dinosaurs?

Jesus lived on earth long after the dinosaurs and about two thousand years before the invention of the Internet.

Animals that did live during the days of the Bible and Jesus' life on earth included camels, donkeys, sheep, goats, dogs, cattle, oxen, horses, lions, bears, hyenas, foxes, monkeys, apes, fish, lizards, snakes, cranes, storks, sparrows, peacocks, ostriches, quail, roosters, chickens, locusts, ants, bees, frogs, flies, fleas, and gnats! In fact, there were so many insects in the Nile Valley, it was called the "land of whirring wings" (Isaiah 18:1).

Who Was John the Baptist?

John the Baptist was Jesus' cousin. John's mother was Elizabeth, a cousin and good friend of Jesus' mother Mary. Like Mary, Elizabeth loved and trusted God.

John was a prophet of God. A prophet is a person who speaks the true word of God to people. The word *prophet* means one who speaks openly. John's mission in life was to tell people that Jesus truly was God's Son (John 1:15, 34).

John loved God with all his heart, mind, and soul. When John grew up, he told people to turn away from their sins. He told them to get ready for Jesus, who was coming soon. Some people thought John was crazy. But many others believed John and turned away from their sins. To show they had turned away from their sins, the people asked John to baptize or dip them in water. The water symbolized the washing away of their sins. Because John baptized people, he became known as "John the Baptist" (Matthew 3:1–12; Mark 1:1–8; Luke 3:1–20; John 1:6–8, 19–28).

The most important person John baptized was Jesus.

When John baptized Jesus, God's Holy Spirit came down from heaven like a dove. Then God's voice said out loud to Jesus, "You are my Son, whom I love; with you I am well pleased" (see Matthew 3:13–17; Mark 1:9–11; Luke 3:21–22). This marked the beginning of Jesus' mission on earth. For the next three years, until His death on the cross, Jesus would preach and teach the message of God's love.

Who Did Jesus Say He Was?

The high priest asked Jesus, "Are you the Christ, the Son of the blessed God?" Jesus answered, "I am" (Mark 14:61–62 NCV).

The apostle John was one of Jesus' best friends. John walked, talked, laughed, and cried with Jesus. He knew Jesus very well. In his Gospel, John wrote what have come to be known as the seven great "I Am" sayings of Jesus.

Here is the list of seven sayings:

➡ **"I am the bread of life."** (John 6:35)

➡ **"I am the light of the world."** (John 8:12)

➡ **"I am the gate for the sheep."** (John 10:7)

➡ **"I am the good shepherd."** (John 10:11)

➡ **"I am the resurrection and the life."** (John 11:25)

➡ **"I am the way and the truth and the life."** (John 14:6)

➡ **"I am the true vine."** (John 15:1)

Why Did Jesus Do Miracles?

Jesus did not do miracles to show off or to entertain people. Jesus did not do miracles for money. Jesus did miracles to show people what God is like.

Because God is loving, Jesus did only loving, kindhearted miracles. He made many sick people well. He healed a twelve-year-old girl (Mark 5:21–42). He healed the apostle Peter's mother-in-law from a fever (Mark 1:29–31). He made lame people walk (John 5:2–9). He made blind people see (Matthew 9:27–30; 20:30–34). He made deaf people hear (Mark 7:31–37). Once, He even brought His dead friend Lazarus back to life! (John 11:1–44).

Jesus did miracles so that people would believe that He really, truly was God's Son

(John 20:30–31).

Jesus did miracles to show how much God loves and cares for His children—and that includes *you* (1 John 3:1)!

Did Jesus Really Feed Five Thousand People with Five Loaves of Bread and Two Fish?

Yes, Jesus really did feed five thousand men, plus women and children, with only five loaves of bread and two fish. He took the loaves and fish, looked up to heaven, and thanked God for what they had—even though it didn't seem to be enough. Then Jesus broke the loaves. When the people had finished eating and were full, the disciples picked up twelve basketfuls of broken pieces that were left over (Matthew 14:13–21)!

? Why did Jesus do this miracle?

➡ Because the **people** were **hungry.** Jesus also did it to teach His disciples to **trust God** to meet their **needs.**

God may not always give you what you want.

But you can trust that God will always give you what you need.

52

Did Jesus Really Walk on Water?

Yes, Jesus really did walk on water.

The Bible tells us that on the same day Jesus fed five thousand people with five loaves of bread and two fish, He went up into the hills by Himself to pray. When evening came, the boat with the disciples was far from land. It was being rocked by the wind and waves. At about three o'clock in the morning, Jesus went out to the disciples, walking on the water. When the disciples saw Him walking on the lake, they were terrified.

"It's a ghost!" they cried out in fear.

But Jesus said, "Take courage! It is I. Don't be afraid."

"Lord, if it's You," said the apostle Peter, "tell me to come to You on the water."

"Come," Jesus said.

Peter lowered himself down out of the boat and walked on the water to Jesus. But when he felt the wind and saw the waves, he was afraid and began to sink.

"Lord, save me!" Peter cried.

Immediately Jesus reached out His hand and caught Peter. "Oh, Peter," He said. "You of little faith. Why did you doubt?"

Then Jesus helped Peter into the boat, and the wind calmed down.

All the disciples were amazed and said to Jesus, "Truly You are the Son of God" (see Matthew 14:22–33).

Jesus did not walk on water to show off. He walked on water to show Peter how powerful faith can be and how important it is to keep your eyes on Jesus. Peter had the beginnings of faith. He even walked on water. But when he took his eyes off Jesus, he lost his faith and sank.

You might think that after seeing Jesus do so many miracles, Peter and the disciples would have lots of faith. Sometimes they did. But sometimes they didn't. This is because Peter and the disciples were regular people, just like you and me.

What Other Things Besides Miracles Did Jesus Do to Show Us What God Is Like?

When people were sad, Jesus cried with them (John 11:35). When people were happy, He laughed with them (John 2:1–2). When people were slow to understand Him, He was very patient (John 20:24–29). When people made mistakes, He forgave them (Luke 23:34).

When Jesus made a promise, He kept it.

He was a loyal and trustworthy friend (John 15:15).

Jesus did all these things to show how much God loves and cares for His children — and that includes *you* (1 John 3:1)!

What Did Jesus Look Like?

Because there were no photographs when Jesus walked and talked on earth, we don't know for sure what He looked like. But we can guess about several of His physical features.

Because Jesus was from Israel, He probably had dark hair and brown eyes. It is likely that Jesus wore His hair long with a dark, uncut beard. Because Jesus worked as a carpenter, He probably had strong, muscular arms (Mark 6:3). Because people liked to be with Jesus, we can assume He laughed and smiled a lot. Because Jesus loved people, He must have had very kind eyes.

What Did Jesus Wear?

We know from the Bible that Jesus wore a *tunic*, or undergarment that was one long piece without a seam (John 19:23). Over His tunic, Jesus wore a loose, flowing *mantle,* or coat. Scholars say the mantle was worn for warmth. It was most likely plain blue, or it may have been white with brown stripes. At the four corners of Jesus' mantle there may have been tassels or fringe.

Around His waist, Jesus wore a *girdle*, or tie. Most girdles were made of leather, about six inches wide, with clasps. A more valuable girdle was made of linen or silk. The girdle also served as a pouch to carry money and small objects.

It is unlikely Jesus wore any jewelry. He may have carried a cane or staff with some decoration on top made of carved wood or hammered metal. Since most people during Jesus' time wore leather sandals, He probably did too (Matthew 10:10; Mark 6:9; Luke 10:4; 22:35).

Did Jesus Have Any Brothers or Sisters?

The Bible tells us that Jesus had four brothers. They were Mary and Joseph's sons, born after Jesus. Jesus also had sisters, but we don't know how many (Matthew 13:55; Mark 6:3).

Jesus' brothers and sisters did not always believe in Him while He was alive on earth (Mark 3:21, 31–35; John 7:5). But after His resurrection and ascension to heaven, Jesus' brothers (and possibly His sisters) were very active in the early church (Acts 1:14). The New Testament includes a letter written by Jesus' brother James.

Who Were the Twelve Apostles?

The twelve apostles were the twelve men Jesus personally selected to be His disciples, or students, while He walked and talked on earth. The twelve original apostles are: Simon (whom Jesus called Peter), and his brother, Andrew, James and his brother, John, Philip, Bartholomew, Thomas, Matthew, James the son of Alphaeus, Thaddaeus (or Jude), Simon the Zealot, and Judas Iscariot (Matthew 10:2–4; Mark 3:16–19; Luke 6:13–16; Acts 1:13).

The twelve apostles were ordinary people, just like you and me. They were not educated, rich, or powerful. But through knowing and loving Jesus, they became extraordinary people. Filled with God's Holy Spirit, they traveled tirelessly by foot and ship, risking their lives to share the story of Jesus with everyone they met. Preaching the good news about Jesus, they changed the world forever.

Here is some information about the twelve apostles. The Bible tells us more about some than others.

Simon, was given the name **Peter** by Jesus (Mark 3:16). Peter was the brother of Andrew and was from the town of Bethsaida on the west coast of the Sea of Galilee (John 1:44). We know Peter was married, because Jesus healed his mother-in-law (Mark 1:29–31). In addition to changing his name, Jesus changed Peter from a fisherman to a "fisher of men" (Matthew 4:19). Sometimes Peter got into trouble by speaking or acting a bit too quickly. On the night Jesus was arrested, Peter became so angry; he cut off the high priest's servant's ear! (John 18:10). Later that night, Peter said three times that he did not know Jesus (John 18:15–17, 25–27). But Jesus loved Peter just the same.

Andrew was Peter's brother, and he was also a fisherman on the Sea of Galilee. He was very good at introducing people to Jesus. In fact, Andrew was the person who first introduced his brother Peter to Jesus!

James was the older brother of John. Their father was Zebedee. James was probably from the town of Capernaum and was also a fisherman in the Sea of Galilee. James, Peter, and John were among Jesus' very best friends. James was present with Peter and John at the Transfiguration (Matthew 17:1), the raising of Jairus's daughter (Mark 5:37–43), and in the Garden of Gethsemane (Mark 14:33)

John was the younger brother of James. Like his brother, he was a fisherman from the Sea of Galilee. Jesus' affectionate nickname for John and James was "Sons of thunder" (Mark 3:17). John and James had very big voices and bold personalities! Over time, John became very close to Jesus. Some people think John was Jesus' best friend. John described himself as "the disciple whom Jesus loved" (John 21:7, 20), and he became a leader in the early church. In addition to his Gospel, John wrote three letters in the New Testament and the book of Revelation.

Philip, like Peter and Andrew, was from Bethsaida (John 1:44).

Bartholomew is thought to have been among the disciples to whom Jesus appeared after His resurrection at the Sea of Tiberias (John 21:2). Bartholomew was also one of the eleven apostles who saw Jesus go back to heaven (Acts 1:1–13).

Thomas was also called Didymus, which is the Greek version of his name. He became known as "doubting Thomas," because he would not believe that Jesus had been raised from the dead until he could see Jesus' resurrected body with his own eyes. When Thomas reached out his hands and touched Jesus' wounds, he said, "My Lord and my God!" Then Jesus said to Thomas, "Because you have seen me, you have believed; blessed are those who have not seen and yet have believed" (John 20:28–29). Thanks to Thomas, Jesus says that we are blessed!

Matthew was a tax collector. Because he collected money for the Romans, nobody liked him! When Matthew met Jesus, he stopped being a tax collector and instead followed Jesus everywhere. Through Jesus, Matthew learned how to love and soon had many friends. He is believed to be the author of the first Gospel in the New Testament.

James was the son of Alphaeus. He was also known as James the Less, possibly because he was younger or shorter than James the brother of John.

Thaddaeus was also known as **Jude** or "Judas son of James" (Luke 6:16; Acts 1:13). In his Gospel in the New Testament, John refers to Thaddaeus as "Judas" 'not' Judas Iscariot" (John 14:22; emphasis added).

Simon the Zealot was a disciple with strong political views. The Zealots were a group of Jews who hoped for an earthly king to restore the nation of Israel to its former glory. But Simon did not let his political views get in the way of his love for Jesus (Matthew 10:4).

Judas Iscariot was another disciple who hoped that Jesus would be an earthly king. But Judas was a traitor who betrayed Jesus. Judas felt so guilty for his act of betrayal that he hanged himself (Matthew 27:3–10).

What's the Difference Between a Disciple and an Apostle?

The word *disciple* means pupil or student. Everyone who is a student or follower of Jesus is a disciple. Because you are a follower of Jesus, *you* are a disciple!

The word *apostle* means one who is sent out.

When Jesus selected His twelve apostles, it was for a special purpose. It was to *send* them to spread the good news of God's love all over the world (Matthew 28:16–20).

The fact that today, more than two thousand years later, the story of Jesus is still being told shows that the apostles did a very good job!

What Was the Transfiguration of Jesus?

One day Jesus took His disciples Peter, James, and John up a high mountain. Suddenly, Jesus' clothes became glistening white. His face shone like the sun. The Bible says that Jesus, in the most extraordinary way, was *transfigured*, or changed in form and appearance.

At the same time, two of the most important men from the Old Testament, Moses and Elijah, appeared. Moses was the lawgiver to whom God gave the Ten Commandments. Elijah was a prophet. They stood there, talking to Jesus.

Suddenly, a bright cloud covered them, and God's voice said, "This is my Son, whom I love; with him I am well pleased. Listen to him!" (Matthew 17:5). When Peter, James, and John heard this, they fell facedown on the ground, terrified.

Jesus bent down to touch them and said, "Get up. Don't be afraid" (Matthew 17:7). When his friends looked up, Moses and Elijah were gone. Jesus told Peter, James, and John to wait until He had been raised from the dead before telling anyone what they had seen (Matthew 17:1–9; Mark 9:2–10; Luke 9:28–36).

The event made a big impression on Peter, James, and John. Later, Peter wrote that he had been an actual eyewitness to the transfiguration of Jesus (2 Peter 1:16–18).

Why Does Jesus Love Children So Much?

Though Jesus never got married or had children of His own, He deeply loved all the boys and girls He met. And the children loved Him back. Grown-ups, Jesus said, could learn a lot from children. Children, He explained, had a simple faith that pleased God.

One day, people were bringing their children to Jesus to have Him bless them. The disciples thought this was silly and told the people to go away.

But Jesus was very upset with His disciples for telling people to take their children away! He said, "Let the little children come to me, and do not hinder them, for the kingdom of God belongs to such as these. I tell you the truth, anyone who will not receive the kingdom of God like a little child will never enter it" (Mark 10:13–16; Luke 18:15–17).

Then Jesus gathered the children in His big, strong arms and blessed them.

Who Was Judas Iscariot?

Judas Iscariot was one of Jesus' twelve original apostles. Jesus called Judas to follow Him, and Judas agreed. Judas was looking for a powerful earthly king for God's people. Judas hoped Jesus was that king. The more Jesus talked about love and forgiveness, the more frustrated and angry Judas became. Judas wasn't interested in love and forgiveness.

The other disciples trusted Judas enough to put him in charge of taking care of their money. Some people say that it was Judas's love of money that made him betray Jesus. Others say Judas was frustrated because Jesus was not the king. Judas wanted Him to be. Whatever the reason, Judas's heart turned evil. For a payment of thirty silver coins, Judas agreed to turn Jesus over to the chief priests who wanted to kill Him (Matthew 26:14–16).

In the dark of night, Judas led the crowd of priests and soldiers to Jesus and His disciples. Earlier, Judas had told the priests that he would let them know who Jesus was by giving Him a kiss (Matthew 26:47–56; Mark 14:43–50; Luke 22:47–53; John 18:1–11). But Jesus knew all along that Judas would betray Him (John 6:64, 70–71). He asked, "Judas, are you betraying the Son of Man with a kiss?" (Luke 22:48). Immediately, Judas knew he had made a terrible mistake. He tried to give the thirty silver coins back, but it was too late. Judas felt so guilty for betraying Jesus that he hanged himself (Matthew 27:3–10).

After Jesus' death, resurrection, and ascension, the original eleven apostles met to pick a disciple to replace Judas. They prayed to God for guidance and picked a man named Matthias (Acts 1:21–26).

Why Did Jesus Have to Die?

Many people understood and believed that Jesus truly was God's Son. They understood and believed what Jesus taught about God's great love for His children. But many others didn't. Some people thought Jesus was crazy. Others thought He was lying. Still others said it was against the law for Jesus to say that God was His Father.

So when Jesus was still a young man, just thirty-three years old, He was killed. Jesus was crucified, or put to death by hanging on a wooden cross. The word *crucify* means to attach to a cross. It was a terrible, painful way to die (Matthew 27; Mark 15; Luke 23; John 19; Acts 2:23; Philippians 2:8).

Jesus was killed by fearful, angry people who didn't understand the things He said and did on earth. Jesus was killed by people who couldn't find it in their hearts to have faith in Him, and in His Father God.

Did Jesus Know Ahead of Time That He Was Going to Die?

Several times Jesus told His disciples that He was going to die. But each time He mentioned His death, the disciples cried, "No! Don't say such a thing!" Jesus also told His disciples ahead of time that He was going to rise from the dead. This was impossible for the disciples to understand (Matthew 17:22–23; 20:17–19; Mark 8:31–39; 9:30-32; 10:32–34; Luke 9:43–45; 18:31–34).

Jesus told His disciples ahead of time about His death and resurrection for a special reason.

It was so that when these things happened, the disciples would remember what Jesus said and would believe (Luke 24:8; John 14:29).

If Jesus Is God's Son, Why Didn't He Save Himself from Being Killed?

Since Jesus is God's Son, He could have stopped the people from killing Him, but He didn't. This is because more than anything, Jesus wanted to be obedient to His Father God in heaven. Jesus was obedient because He loved and trusted God.

On the night before He was put to death, Jesus went to a garden called Gethsemane to pray. He was very sad and troubled. Jesus loved life. He did not want to die. Jesus fell with His face to the ground and cried out to God.

"Abba, Father," He said, "everything is possible for you. Take this cup from me. Yet not what I will, but what you will" (Mark 14:36). When Jesus said, "Abba," He meant daddy or papa. When Jesus said, "Take this cup," He meant that His death would be like drinking a cup of poison.

Jesus chose to be obedient and do His Father's will.

By choosing to be obedient and give up His life, Jesus took upon Himself the punishment for all the bad things people do and think (1 John 2:2).

Jesus died to save everyone who would believe in Him. That is why He is called our Savior.

What Are the Seven Sayings of Jesus on the Cross?

When Jesus was on the cross, the four Gospels record Him saying seven sentences before He died. Jesus spoke to His mother. Jesus spoke to His disciples. Jesus spoke to a criminal who was being put to death on a cross next to Him. Jesus also spoke to His Father God.

Because Jesus was in great pain, facing death, and about to take upon Himself the sins of all human beings, these words reveal a lot about Jesus. They tell us what is important to Him. Over the years, these words have come to be known as the Seven Sayings of Jesus on the Cross.

They are listed for you here.

1. "Father, forgive them, for they do not know what they are doing" (Luke 23:34). Jesus said this to God about the soldiers at the bottom of the cross. The soldiers were casting lots to see who would get Jesus' clothes after He died. Even on the cross, Jesus was loving and forgiving. Even on the cross, Jesus kept talking to His Father God.

2. "I tell you the truth, today you will be with me in paradise" (Luke 23:43). Jesus said this to a criminal hanging on the cross next to Him. The criminal had recognized Jesus as God's Son. Because the criminal believed in Jesus, Jesus forgave him for his sins. Jesus promised that when the criminal died, he would be with Jesus in paradise. When Jesus said "paradise", He meant heaven.

3. "When Jesus saw his mother there, and the disciple whom he loved standing nearby, he said to his mother, 'Dear woman, here is your son,' and to the disciple, 'Here is your mother'" (John 19:26–27). Jesus loved His mother very much. He wanted to be sure that she would be taken care of after He died. Jesus asked the disciple John to take care of Mary. John loved Jesus, and he took Mary to live with him in his home as though she were his own mother (see John 19:25–27).

4. "My God, my God, why have you forsaken me?'" (Matthew 27:46; Mark 15:34). Jesus said this to God during the terrible time He was taking all the sins of the world upon His human body. It was the time when Jesus felt totally cut off and separated from His Father God. It was the darkest, most horrible time in Jesus' life.

5. "I am thirsty" (John 19:28). Jesus was God's Son, but He was also human. The cross was a terrible way to die. Jesus was in great pain. Jesus was thirsty.

6. "Father, into your hands I commit my spirit" (Luke 23:46). Jesus said this in a loud voice. Although Jesus suffered, He never stopped believing in God. He never stopped trusting God. Before Jesus died, He willingly gave God His spirit.

7. "It is finished" (John 19:30). Jesus died knowing He had been obedient to God's will. With these words, Jesus completed His mission on earth. Jesus took upon Himself the sins of the whole world. Jesus died to save all who would believe in Him.

> **Jesus died for me and for you.**

What Happened to Jesus' Body?

One of Jesus' disciples was a rich man named Joseph of Arimathea. After Jesus was crucified, Joseph got permission from the Roman authorities to take and bury the lifeless body of Jesus.

Joseph and his friend Nicodemus wrapped Jesus' body in clean linen cloth. Between the strips of linen, they inserted fragrant spices. Then they laid Jesus' body gently in a tomb (Matthew 27:57–60; Mark 15:42–46; Luke 23: 50–53; John 19:38–42). Back then, a *tomb* was a small, dark room with a dirt floor, carved into rock.

Jesus' mother, Mary, was there. So was Mary Magdalene, another friend of Jesus'. After they laid Jesus' body in the tomb, Joseph rolled a big stone over the opening of the tomb (Matthew 27:57–61). And then—their hearts breaking with sorrow—they all walked away.

How shocked and sad people were on the day Jesus died! His mother and brothers and sisters and disciples all missed Him terribly. They cried and cried. *If only Jesus could somehow come back and be with us*, they thought. But that was impossible. Never again would they hear the sound of Jesus' laughter. Never again would they listen to His stories, or feel His big, strong hugs.

Or so they thought . . .

What Was the Resurrection of Jesus?

Three days after Jesus died, early in the morning of the first day of the week, Mary Magdalene and Jesus' mother, Mary, set off to visit the tomb where Jesus' body had been laid. But when they arrived, the big stone that covered the opening to the tomb had been rolled away. The tomb was empty!

Where has the body of our beloved Jesus gone? the women wondered.

Moments later, they made a wonderful, important, extraordinary discovery: Jesus was *alive!* The tomb was empty because Jesus—in the most awesome, miraculous way—was no longer dead, *but had come back to life!*

As fast as their legs could carry them, Mary Magdalene and Mary ran to tell the disciples the good news.

The word *resurrect* means to bring back to life or raise from the dead.

Each of the four Gospels reports different, exciting details about Jesus' resurrection. For the most complete account of what happened when Jesus was resurrected, it's best to read all four Gospel reports (Matthew 28:1–10; Mark 16:1–8; Luke 24:1–12; John 20:1–18).

Why Is Jesus' Resurrection So Important?

After Jesus' resurrection, He explained that soon He would be going back to heaven to live with His Father God. But before He left, He had some very good news.

Everyone leaned forward and listened carefully.

"The good news," said Jesus, "is that because I have come back to life, you can too. After you die, you can live forever with My Father God and Me in heaven. God loves you so much, He wants this for you. God wants you to believe in Him and Me. God wants to forgive your sins. God wants you to live in heaven forever" (see John 3:16). Jesus explained to His family and disciples that because they loved and believed in Him, after their life on earth ended, they would find themselves alive in heaven.

What a happy place heaven is! It's like a big birthday party. This is because everyone in heaven is happy and healthy. Everyone in heaven has new bodies that live forever, and there is no more death or sadness or crying or pain. In heaven, God will wipe away every tear from every eye (Revelation 7:17).

The **resurrection** of Jesus is important because it means that our sins can be **forgiven.** Because **you believe** in Jesus, you can **live forever** with God and Jesus in **heaven!**

How Can I Know for Sure That Jesus Really Was Resurrected?

The resurrection of Jesus is not a legend, myth, or fairy tale. It is a true historical fact. Here is the order in which the resurrected Jesus appeared to eyewitnesses:

1. The first people to see the resurrected Jesus were His friend, Mary Magdalene; His mother, Mary; and other women (Matthew 28:1–9; Mark 16:9–10; John 20:11–18).

2. Jesus appeared to two disciples on the road to the village Emmaus (Mark 16:12; Luke 24:13–15).

3. Jesus appeared to the disciple Simon Peter in Jerusalem (Luke 24:34; 1 Corinthians 15:5).

4. Jesus appeared to ten disciples, excluding Thomas, in the upper room in Jerusalem (John 20:19).

5. One week later Jesus appeared to the eleven disciples in the upper room, including Thomas. Thomas was so unsure about the Resurrection that he became known as "doubting Thomas." But when Thomas saw the resurrected Jesus with his own eyes and put his fingers in the scars of Jesus' wounds, he believed (Mark 16:14; Luke 24:36; John 20:26–28).

6. Jesus appeared to seven disciples at the Sea of Tiberias (John 21:1–14).

7. Jesus appeared to the eleven disciples on a mountain in Galilee (Matthew 28:16–20).

8. Jesus appeared to five hundred other eyewitnesses (1 Corinthians 15:6).

9. Jesus appeared to the disciple James (1 Corinthians 15:7).

10. Jesus appeared to all those who witnessed His ascension into heaven (Mark 16:19; Luke 24:50–51; Acts 1:3–12).

What Was the Ascension of Christ?

Jesus walked and talked on earth in His resurrected body for forty days. Then He gathered His disciples on the Mount of Olives near Bethany. The time had come for Jesus to join His Father God in heaven.

Before Jesus left the earth, He told the disciples to preach the good news of God's love to all creation (Matthew 28:18-20; Mark 16:15; Acts 1:8). He also told the disciples to stay in the city until they "received that power from heaven" (Luke 24:49 NCV). By "power from heaven," Jesus meant the arrival of the Holy Spirit. This would happen later in Jerusalem (Acts 2:1–4).

Then Jesus was "taken up into heaven and he sat at the right hand of God" (Mark 16:19).

The word *ascension* means the act of going up.

As Jesus went up to heaven, the Bible says that a cloud hid Jesus from the disciples' sight (Acts 1:9).

What Is the Great Commission?

These are among the last words Jesus told His disciples before ascending to heaven to join His Father God: "All authority in heaven and on earth has been given to me. Therefore go and make disciples of all nations, baptizing them in the name of the Father and of the Son and of the Holy Spirit, and teaching them to obey everything I have commanded you. And surely I am with you always, to the very end of the age" (Matthew 28:18–20; see also Mark 16:15).

Over the years, this powerful command has become known as the Great Commission. The word *commission* means authority that is given to someone. Jesus' last words on earth granted authority to the disciples to go out and tell the whole world about God's love through Jesus.

> ## Today this is our commission too.
> Jesus wants us, each in our own way, to let the world know about God's love.

What Is the Second Coming of Christ?

While the disciples were gazing up in wonder at Jesus' ascension into heaven, two angels in white robes appeared. "'Men of Galilee'," they said, "'why do you stand here looking into the sky? This same Jesus, who has been taken from you into heaven, will come back in the same way you have seen him go into heaven'" (Acts 1:10–11).

Jesus said, "And you will see the Son of Man sitting at the right hand of the Mighty One and coming on the clouds of heaven" (Mark 14:62). When Jesus said "the Son of Man," He meant Himself. When He said "the Mighty One," He meant God.

Jesus will come again someday. When Jesus comes back, everyone will recognize that He is God's Son. He will come "in the clouds." He will come with God's holy angels (Mark 8:38). For people who believe in Jesus, this will be a happy time!

Jesus will gather us all in His big, strong arms. Our hearts will be filled with joy!

No one knows for sure when Jesus will return. Not even the angels. Only God in heaven knows for sure (Mark 13:32–37).

How should we prepare for the second coming of Jesus? Jesus answered this question with one word: "Watch!" (Mark 13:36).

While we watch and wait, Jesus wants us to live our lives as though He were coming back today. Jesus wants us to love God. Jesus wants us to love each other.

Love is the key.

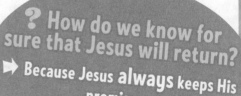

? How do we know for sure that Jesus will return?

➡ Because Jesus **always** keeps His promises.

(Deuteronomy 7:9; 1 Corinthians 1:9).

Why Couldn't Jesus Just Stay on Earth Forever?

Jesus told His family and friends that although He could no longer stay with them on earth, there was a special way that He could live with them in their hearts.

"It is for your good that I am going away," said Jesus (see John 16:7). "When I go, God will send you His Holy Spirit. The Holy Spirit will live in your hearts and guide you. He will comfort you. He will lead you to truth. He will help you remember everything I have taught you. He will give you the power to love others the way I have loved you" (see John 14:15–26; 16:7–15).

A few days after Jesus' ascension to heaven, the disciples gathered in Jerusalem. The Holy Spirit arrived and filled the hearts of the disciples. Though Jesus was no longer with them in person, He was alive in their hearts! (Acts 2:1–4).

Through the Holy Spirit, Jesus can live in the hearts of lots of people, in lots of places.

Thanks to the Holy Spirit, the message of God's love can travel all over the world.

Can Anyone Believe in Jesus?

God loves all His children and wants them all to believe in Him and in His Son, Jesus. The Bible says, "Everyone who calls on the name of the Lord will be saved" (Acts 2:21). Yes, anyone can believe in Jesus. But God does not force His children to love Him. It's up to everyone, each on their own, to have faith in Jesus.

The good news is that it's never too late to believe in God and in His Son, Jesus. You can be ten years old or one hundred years old. God is very patient and forgiving. God is always waiting with open arms for His children to come to Him.

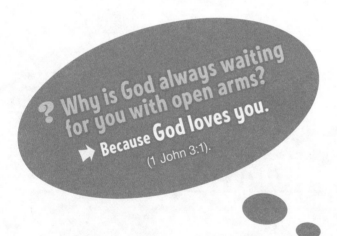

? Why is God always waiting for you with open arms?

➤ Because God loves you.

(1 John 3:1).

How Do I Get to Know Jesus?

The best way to get to know Jesus is to talk to Him. Tell Him that you want to get to know Him better. Jesus is always ready to hear your prayers.

Just pray, "Jesus, I really want to know You. I believe You are the Son of God. I believe that You died for my sins. Thank You for loving me so much. Now please come into my heart and live in me."

When Jesus lives in your heart, He will help you tell right from wrong.

He will forgive you when you make mistakes (1 John 1:9). He will comfort you when you are feeling down. He will be your very best friend (John 15:15).

? How can you be sure Jesus will come into your heart?
➡ Because Jesus said He would, and He always, always keeps His promises.
(1 Thessalonians 5:24; Hebrews 10:23).

? Why does Jesus want to do all this for you?
➡ Because Jesus **loves** you.
(John 15:9, 13; 1 John 3:16)

Who Is the Holy Spirit?

The Holy Spirit is the third Person of the Trinity. The Holy Spirit is not just an idea. He is a powerful, living Person! The Holy Spirit is the way God lives in the hearts of human beings. The Holy Spirit is the way God lives in *your* heart.

In the Old Testament, God's Holy Spirit was known as the giver of life, and as the One who spoke God's Word through the prophets. In the New Testament, the Holy Spirit is described as God's love, poured into our hearts (Romans 5:5).

"God will send you His Holy Spirit," Jesus told the disciples. "He will live in your hearts and guide you. He will comfort you. He will lead you to truth. He will help you remember everything I have taught you. He will give you the power to love others the way I have loved you" (see John 14:15–26; 16:7–15).

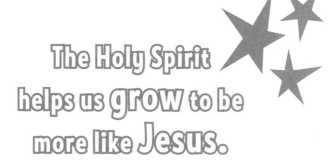

The Holy Spirit helps us grow to be more like Jesus.

The Holy Spirit opens our minds to understanding God's Word in the Bible. The Holy Spirit allows God to accomplish His work on earth right this very minute.

How loving God is to fill us with His Holy Spirit!

How Does the Holy Spirit Help Me?

The Holy Spirit gives you God's special power to love (Romans 5:5).

The Holy Spirit is like a battery in a flashlight. Without a battery, a flashlight looks just fine on the outside. But when it's dark and you need to use it, it doesn't work.

A flashlight with a battery looks the same on the outside as the flashlight without a battery. But when it's dark, and you need to use it, it works. The flashlight with a battery shines the light into the darkness. It shows you where you are going. It protects you from stumbling or falling. It might even save your life!

God's Holy Spirit is like your spiritual battery.

The Holy Spirit gives you the power to tell right from wrong. He gives you the power to care more about other people. He gives you the power to think and act more like Jesus. He gives you special power to shine the light of God's love in the world.

Is the Holy Ghost Really a Ghost?

The Holy Ghost is not a ghost! *Holy Ghost* is simply an old-fashioned name for the *Holy Spirit* (see the King James Version of Matthew 1:20; Mark 1:8; Luke 3:22; John 14:26; Acts 2:4).

The word *spirit* means breath. When God's Holy Spirit lives in your heart, He allows God to breathe through you. The word *ghost* also means spirit, but today we often think of a ghost as the spirit of a dead person. God is *not* a dead person!

> **Holy Ghost comes from a translation of the Bible called the King James Version.**

The King James Version of the Bible was written about four hundred years ago, in 1611.Some people think it is one of the most beautiful books ever written.

There are other translations of the Bible that are easier to understand, but some Christians still use the King James Version of the Bible and prefer to call the Holy Spirit the Holy Ghost.

What Are the Gifts of the Holy Spirit?

The Holy Spirit gives you the power to think and act like Jesus. When Jesus walked and talked on earth, He did a lot of loving things. He healed the sick. He gave sight to the blind. He fed the hungry. He comforted people who were lonely. He felt other people's pain. He warned about things that would happen in the future. Jesus did all these things to show us how much God loves us.

The purpose of the gifts of the Holy Spirit is to help us love and help each other—just like Jesus did when He was on earth.

Here is what the apostle Paul wrote about the gifts of the Holy Spirit:

Now to each one the manifestation of the Spirit is given for the common good. To one there is given through the Spirit the *message of wisdom*, to another the *message of knowledge* by means of the same Spirit, to another *faith* by the same Spirit, to another *gifts of healing* by that one Spirit, to another *miraculous powers*, to another *prophecy*, to another *distinguishing between spirits*, to another *speaking in different kinds of tongues*, and to still another the *interpretation of tongues*. All these are the work of one and the same Spirit, and he gives them to each one, just as he determines. (1 Corinthians 12:7–11; emphasis added)

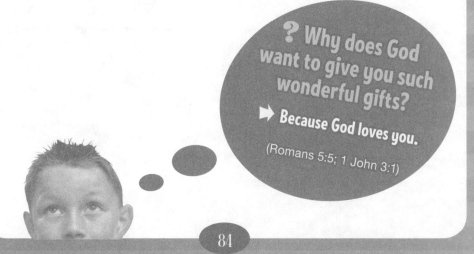

? Why does God want to give you such wonderful gifts?

➜ **Because God loves you.**

(Romans 5:5; 1 John 3:1)

What Is the Most Important Gift of the Holy Spirit?

The purpose of the Holy Spirit is to help you think and act like Jesus. The way that Jesus thinks and acts can be summed up in one word: *love*. Why is this? Because God is love (1 John 4:8).

The word *love* means to care for. The word *love* is used in a lot of different ways. You can love riding your bike. You can love chocolate-chip cookie dough ice cream. You can love your dog. You can love your friend. You can love your grandma and grandpa.

Christian love is caring for another human being as much as you care for yourself. The apostle Paul described Christian love this way: "Love is patient, love is kind. It does not envy, it does not boast, it is not proud. It is not rude, it is not self-seeking, it is not easily angered, it keeps no record of wrongs. Love does not delight in evil but rejoices with the truth. It always protects, always trusts, always hopes, always perseveres. Love never fails" (1 Corinthians 13:4–8).

The apostle Paul believed that of all the gifts of the Holy Spirit, the greatest gift is *love* (1 Corinthians 13:13). It is interesting to note that Christian love is not just a feeling. Christian love is feelings put into action.

What Is the Fruit of the Holy Spirit?

When the Holy Spirit lives in your heart, others can tell. This is because the Holy Spirit changes you. The Holy Spirit produces outward, visible signs that He is living in you and helping you be more like Jesus.

These outward signs of the Holy Spirit are sometimes called "fruit." They are called fruit, because fruit is an outward sign of a healthy, living plant. Fruit is beautiful to look at. Fruit is delicious to eat. Fruit nourishes the body. The fruit that the Holy Spirit produces is an outward sign of a healthy soul.

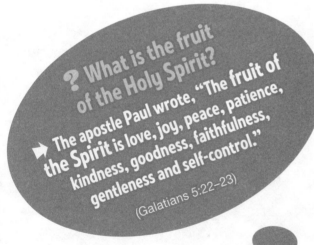

? What is the fruit of the Holy Spirit?

➤ The apostle Paul wrote, "The fruit of the Spirit is love, joy, peace, patience, kindness, goodness, faithfulness, gentleness and self-control."

(Galatians 5:22–23)

What Is the Bible?

The Bible is the most important book in the world. Why? Because the Bible is the true, inspired Holy Word of God. The apostle Paul described the Bible as "God-breathed" (2 Timothy 3:16). God breathed through the human beings who wrote the Bible. This is what makes the Bible different from all other books.

When you pick up a Bible, you are holding more than one book. You are actually holding a whole library! This is because the Bible contains sixty-six books, written by forty different people, over a period of about two thousand years. In the Bible you will discover an amazing collection of *real*, true-life stories about kings and queens and angels and giants. You will read *real*, true-life stories of adventure and love, plus poetry, songs, prayers, and letters—even predictions about the future! Best of all, you will read the *real*, true-life story of Jesus, whom God sent to earth to save the world. Talk about exciting!

Remember, the Bible is *not* a dry, boring book. It is the living Word of God! When you read the Bible, you get to know God better. This is because God is able to actually *speak to you* through the Bible. Isn't that amazing?

The Bible also answers the really big questions about life on earth—Who am I? Why am I here? What will happen to me when I die?

> **The Bible is God's special love letter to you!**

How Did We Get the Bible?

In ancient times, many people didn't know how to write or read. They didn't have books. They didn't have TV or computers. They didn't even have paper and pencils! Instead, they told stories.

The Bible begins with the oldest stories about how God created the universe, earth, plants, animals, and the first human beings, Adam and Eve (Genesis 1–3). It tells the story of Noah's ark (Genesis 6–9). It tells the story of the Tower of Babel (Genesis 11:1–9). These very early stories in the Bible were first passed down orally from generation to generation. The word *orally* means by mouth. Parents told their children who told their children.

Since God's stories were so important, people made a special effort to write them down. But in ancient times, the only people able to read and write were called "scribes." The word *scribe* comes from a Latin word which means to write. Most books of the Bible were copied down by scribes on papyrus scrolls (Jeremiah 36:2). Later they were written on parchment. Thanks to the scribes' hard work, the message of God's love spread all over the ancient world. (Ezra 7:12; Psalm 45:1)

In the early church, people who loved God had special meetings called councils to decide which books would be included in the final version of the Bible. Before each council, they prayed for the Holy Spirit to help them choose just the right books.

Then, in the fifteenth century, the mechanical printing press was invented by a man named Johann Gutenberg, in Germany. In 1457, Gutenberg's Bible was the very first complete book ever printed. Gutenberg's Bible was written in Latin, the language of the church. It was printed in two big volumes of 1,282 unnumbered pages!

The word *Bible* comes from the Greek word *biblios*, which means book. But here is an interesting fact: the word *Bible* is not found in the Bible! This is because the term came into use long after all the books of the Bible were completed and selected.

Today the Bible is the world's best-selling book. Over the years, billions of Bibles have been printed. The Bible has been translated into more than two thousand languages!

Thanks to the Bible, people everywhere on earth can learn about God's love.

How Do I Know the Bible Is True?

The Bible is different from any other book in the world. Why? Because it is written by many different people who wrote under the inspiration of God. This does not mean that God dictated His words to the writers. This means that *God breathed His truth into the hearts of the writers*. Through His Holy Spirit, God inspired the writers so they would know just what to write.

God's Holy Spirit is alive today through the pages of every Bible (Hebrews 4:12). The Bible has the power to speak God's truth to the hearts of all human beings. The Bible has the power to speak God's truth to *you*. That is why the Bible is often called "God's Word."

Here is an interesting fact:

The Bible is the most documented and reliable book in the world. Scholars of the Bible have more than *thirteen thousand* manuscript copies of portions of the New Testament, which they continue to study and learn from this very day! Ongoing new discoveries by biblical archeologists also help to prove the Bible's remarkable historical accuracy.

What's the Difference Between the Old Testament and the New Testament?

The books of the Bible are divided into two sections: the Old Testament and the New Testament. The word *testament* means covenant or agreement. In the Bible, the covenant or agreement is between a loving God and His children.

The Old Testament

The Old Testament starts before the beginning of time and covers thousands of years. It is nearly twice as long as the New Testament. In the Old Testament, we learn about God's love for the Jews, the people of Israel. God loved the people of Israel so much they were known as God's "chosen" people (Deuteronomy 7:6).

In the Old Testament, God made a covenant with His people (Genesis 12:2–3, 7; 13:14–17; 21:12, 22:16–18). God expected His people to believe in Him, love Him, and obey His laws (Exodus 20:1–17). This was not easy!

The Old Testament also includes prophecies about God's Son, the Messiah, being born. Most of the Old Testament was written in Hebrew, the language of the people of Israel. Parts of the books of Ezra and Daniel were written in Aramaic, a language similar to Hebrew.

The Old Testament and the New Testament are separated in history by a break of four hundred years.

The New Testament

The New Testament begins with the birth of God's Son, Jesus (Matthew 1:18–25; Luke 2:1–20). Mathew, Mark, Luke, John, and Acts 1 tell about the life, teachings, death, resurrection, and ascension to heaven of Jesus. Acts 2 tells about the arrival of God's Holy Spirit on earth and about the growth of the early church.

Many of the books in the New Testament are letters from people who personally knew Jesus when He walked and talked on earth. The last book of the New Testament is a vision about the future that was written by one of Jesus' best friends, John. The books of the New Testament were originally written in Greek.

In the New Testament, God made a new covenant with His people. Through believing in His Son, Jesus, God invites *everyone* to become one of His "chosen people" (see Romans 8:14). This is good news. Through believing in Jesus, *you* are one of "God's chosen people"!

Books of Law

Genesis
Exodus
Leviticus
Numbers
Deuteronomy

Books of History

Joshua
Judges
Ruth
1 Samuel
2 Samuel
1 Kings
2 Kings
1 Chronicles
2 Chronicles
Ezra
Nehemiah
Esther

Books of Poetry

Job
Psalms
Proverbs
Ecclesiastes
Song of Songs

Books of Prophecy

Isaiah
Jeremiah
Lamentations
Ezekiel
Daniel

Hosea
Joel
Amos
Obadiah
Jonah

Micah
Nahum
Habakkuk
Zephaniah
Haggai

Zechariah
Malachi

Twenty-Seven Books of the New Testament

Gospels

Matthew
Mark
Luke
John

Books of History

Acts

Letters to Christians

Romans
1 Corinthians
2 Corinthians
Galatians
Ephesians
Philippians

Colossians
1 Thessalonians
2 Thessalonians
1 Timothy
2 Timothy
Titus

Philemon
Hebrews
James
1 Peter
2 Peter
1 John

2 John
3 John
Jude

Books of Prophecy

Revelation

What's the Difference Between a Jew and a Gentile?

The word Jew is the most commonly used name for the people of Israel (Jeremiah 32:12). The word *Jew* is derived from the Hebrew word *Yehudi*, meaning "one who comes from Judea." Judea was the ancient region of southern Palestine that was made up of modern-day southern Israel and southwest Jordan. Jews are also sometimes called Israelites or Hebrews.

A **Gentile** is any person who is not Jewish.

Today there are many Gentiles who love God very much!

Why Does God's Name Sometimes Appear as "LORD" in the Old Testament?

God's name was holy to the Jews. It was so holy that the Jews, out of reverence to God, did not write or say His name. This was also done to strictly obey the third commandment: "You shall not misuse the name of the LORD your God" (Exodus 20:7).

The ancient Hebrew alphabet had no written vowels. It also had no lowercase and uppercase letters. In the original Old Testament manuscripts, the name of God was written as four Hebrew consonants, which translate into English as YHWH or JHVH. This grouping of four letters is called the *Tetragrammaton*—which is a very big word!

Some English versions of the Bible add vowels to YHWH and JHVH to create the words *Yahweh* and *Jehovah*. Most Bibles translate YHVH and JHVH as LORD.

Even today, some Jewish people will not write or say the name of God. Instead, they substitute the name *Adonai*, which means "my Lord," or *Ha Shem*, which means "the Name." Some Jewish people write the English word "God" with the middle letter deleted, so it looks like this: "G-d." All this is done out of reverence and a desire to obey God's law.

What Are the Ten Commandments?

More than three thousand years ago, God chose Moses to be the leader of the Jews. Moses loved and obeyed God, and led the Jews out of slavery in Egypt. First they crossed the Red Sea. Then Moses led the Jews on a long and difficult journey into the wilderness. Moses was a good leader, but still the people got in trouble. They needed rules to live by.

God loved His people. He called Moses to the top of Mount Sinai, where He delivered His rules. Over the years, God's rules became known as the Ten Commandments.

Even today, the Ten Commandments form the basis for many of our laws and our ideas of right and wrong.

The Ten Commandments are based on love.

In these commands, we find almost all the moral teachings and wisdom of the Bible. This is why they are *not* called the Ten Suggestions!

The Ten Commandments

1. "You shall have no other gods before me" (Exodus 20:3).

2. "You shall not make for yourself an idol in the form of anything in heaven above or on the earth beneath or in the waters below" (Exodus 20:4).

3. "You shall not misuse the name of the Lord your God" (Exodus 20:7).

4. "Remember the Sabbath day by keeping it holy" (Exodus 20:8).

5. "Honor your father and your mother, so that you may live long in the land the Lord your God is giving you" (Exodus 20:12).

6. "You shall not murder" (Exodus 20:13).

7. "You shall not commit adultery" (Exodus 20:14).

8. "You shall not steal" (Exodus 20:15).

9. "You must not tell lies" (Exodus 20:16 NCV).

10. "You must not be envious" (Exodus 20:17 TLB).

What's the Greatest Commandment?

In the New Testament, Jesus was asked by the religious leaders of His day, "Teacher, which is the greatest commandment in the Law?" Jesus replied,

"Love the Lord your God with all your heart and with all your soul and with all your mind.

This is the first and greatest commandment" (Matthew 22:35–38).

Here is how this commandment appears in the Old Testament: "Hear, O Israel: The LORD our God, the LORD is one. Love the LORD your God with all your heart and with all your soul and with all your strength" (Deuteronomy 6:4–5).

God loves you *so* much!

More than anything, God wants you to know and love Him too.

What Is the Golden Rule?

After Jesus told the religious leaders about the Greatest Commandment, He added a second, very important commandment: "Love your neighbor as yourself" (Matthew 22:39; Mark 12:31).

Over the years, the idea of loving other people the way we would like to be loved has come to be known as the golden rule. It is called "golden" because gold is of great value. The golden rule is of such great value that Jesus mentions it over and over in the Bible. "So in everything, do to others what you would have them do to you," Jesus says (Matthew 7:12). And again, "Do to others as you would have them do to you" (Luke 6:31).

When we show
God's love to others,
we show God
that we **love** Him.

What Are the Psalms?

The psalms are 150 beautiful poems and songs for worship. They were written over many centuries by different authors, including Moses, King David, and King Solomon. The Hebrew name for the book of Psalms was the Book of Praises. This is because so many of the psalms are songs of praise to God (Psalms 18; 100; 103). Although many of the psalms were written almost a thousand years before Jesus, some of them refer to Him! (Psalms 2; 16; 22; 23; 45; 110).

Many of the psalms were written by King David of Israel. God loved David, and King David loved God back. Sometimes David thought his heart would burst, he felt so much love for God. Sometimes King David was sad. Sometimes he was afraid. David wrote psalms to tell God about his feelings.

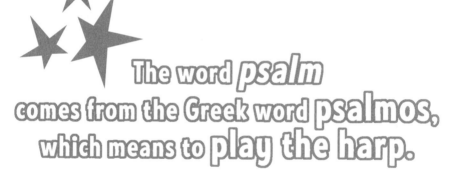

The word *psalm* comes from the Greek word *psalmos*, which means to play the harp.

When we read the psalms, it is easy to imagine the sound of beautiful voices singing. Through the psalms, we, like King David, can sing to God about everything—our fears, our hopes, our joy, our sadness, and our dreams.

The book of Psalms is easy to find—it's right in the middle of the Bible!

Why Does the Word *Selah* Appear in the Margins of the Psalms?

Many of the psalms were written as songs of praise to God. The word *Selah* is a musical sign that means to lift up. It was written in the margins as a direction to the singers to "lift up loud" their voices. It was also a direction to the members of the orchestra to "lift up loud" their instruments.

The word *Selah* appears more than **seventy times** in the book of Psalms. It also appears **three** times in Habakkuk.

What Is the Shepherd's Psalm?

The Twenty-third Psalm is the most famous of all the psalms. It is a beautiful song about God, written by King David of Israel.

King David loved and trusted God with all his heart, just like a sheep trusts a shepherd. When you are worried or sad, the Twenty-third Psalm is a very comforting psalm to read. It also helps us understand what Jesus meant when He said, "I am the good shepherd" (John 10:14).

Psalm 23

The LORD is my shepherd, I shall not be in want.
  He makes me lie down in green pastures,
he leads me beside quiet waters,
  he restores my soul.
He guides me in paths of righteousness
  for his name's sake.
Even though I walk
  through the valley of the shadow of death,
I will fear no evil,
  for you are with me;
your rod and your staff,
  they comfort me.

You prepare a table before me
  in the presence of my enemies.
You anoint my head with oil;
  my cup overflows.
Surely goodness and love will follow me
  all the days of my life,
and I will dwell in the house of the LORD
  forever.

Does the Old Testament Have Anything to Say about Jesus?

God gave lots of exciting clues in the Old Testament about His Son, Jesus, coming to earth. These clues are called prophecies. God gave lots of clues because He wanted His children to be sure to recognize Jesus when He arrived. God sent Jesus to earth to save His children—and that includes *you*!

Finding prophecies about Jesus in the Old Testament is fun. It is like being a detective. Would you like to be a Bible detective? In the chart below are six Old Testament prophecies about Jesus that are fulfilled in the New Testament—though there are many more. Open up your Bible, and have fun!

Some Old Testament Prophecies Fulfilled in the New Testament

Jesus would be born of a virgin.
(Isaiah 7:14; Matthew 1:23–25)

Jesus would be born in Bethlehem.
(Micah 5:2; Luke 2:4–7)

Jesus would be taken to Egypt.
(Hosea 11:1; Matthew 2:14–15)

Jesus would heal many.
(Isaiah 53:4; Matthew 8:16)

Jesus would die on a cross with sinners.
(Isaiah 53:12; Matthew 27:38)

None of Jesus' bones would be broken.
(Psalm 34:20; John 19:33)

What Are the Four Gospels?

The word *gospel* means good news (see the King James Versions of Matthew 11:5; Luke 4:18; 7:22). The first four books of the New Testament are known as the four Gospels because they tell the good news about Jesus! The four Gospels are Matthew, Mark, Luke, and John. They were written by men who actually walked and talked with Jesus or knew people who did.

Matthew was a tax collector. Because he collected money for the Romans, nobody liked him. When he met Jesus, he stopped being a tax collector and followed Jesus everywhere. Through Jesus, Matthew learned how to love and soon had many friends. Matthew wrote his Gospel around AD 60–70 (about thirty years after Jesus' death). The Gospel of Matthew pays special attention to Jesus' teachings and sermons.

Mark was a teenager when Jesus and His followers met in Mark's mother's house in Jerusalem. Mark watched and listened to Jesus as He taught. Mark's full name was John Mark. He may have been present when Jesus died on the cross. Mark traveled with and learned a lot about Jesus from another disciple named Peter. He also traveled with the apostle Paul and Barnabas. Mark wrote his Gospel around AD 55–65. It is the earliest written and shortest Gospel. The Gospel of Mark pays special attention to Jesus' miracles.

Luke was a Greek-speaking doctor. Luke didn't know Jesus personally, but he carefully researched his life by talking to many people who did know Jesus. He traveled with Paul on some of his missionary trips. Luke also wrote the book of Acts in the New Testament, which tells the story of the early Christian church. Luke wrote his Gospel around AD 60–70. The Gospel of Luke pays special attention to Jesus' parables.

John was a fisherman. When John met Jesus, he became one of the apostles and was the closest to Jesus. Some people think John was Jesus' best friend. John described himself as "the disciple whom Jesus loved" (John 21:7, 20). John became a leader in the early church. In addition to his Gospel, John also wrote three letters in the New Testament. It is believed that he also wrote the book of Revelation. John wrote his Gospel around AD 70–90. The Gospel of John pays special attention to how much God loves us.

If the Gospels Are All about Jesus, Why Are They Different?

Each of the four Gospels tells a slightly different story about Jesus, because they are written by four different people—Matthew, Mark, Luke, and John.

This makes a lot of sense. Imagine that four of your friends wrote a story about you. Some of their stories would be the same. But because each friend knows you in a different way, parts of his or her story would be different. Maybe you went to a birthday party with all four friends. All four would write about the birthday party. But maybe you went ice-skating with only one of the friends. Only that friend would write about ice-skating. All four stories together would give the best, most complete picture of you.

Together, all four Gospels give the best, most complete picture of Jesus.

What Are the Epistles?

The Epistles are a collection of letters in the New Testament. The word *epistle* means to send a message. Another more commonly used word for epistles is *letters*.

The New Testament Letters were written by different men who lived at the same time as Jesus. In fact, some of them actually walked and talked with Jesus! One of the most famous letter writers was the apostle Paul.

The Letters were written to teach and encourage Christians in different places. Some Letters are named after the writer (James; 1 and 2 Peter; 1, 2, and 3 John; Jude). Others are named after the people to whom the letter was written (1 and 2 Timothy; Titus; Philemon; Hebrews). Still other Letters are named after the cities and towns to which the letter was sent (Romans; 1 and 2 Corinthians; Galatians; Ephesians; Philippians; Colossians; 1 and 2 Thessalonians).

Today, the Letters continue to teach and encourage Christians around the world.

What Are the Beatitudes?

The word *beatitude* comes from a Latin word that means happy.

One day after healing many people, Jesus climbed up a mountain. His disciples gathered around Him, and He began to teach. This became known as the Sermon on the Mount (Matthew 5:1–12; Luke 6:20–23). In His Sermon on the Mount, Jesus taught about what makes people truly "blessed," or happy.

Over the years, these nine teachings became known as the Beatitudes. Some people refer to them as the "Be Attitudes," because they teach us how God wants us to be! Remember when you read them that the word *blessed* means happy. They are printed for you here.

Blessed are the poor in spirit,
    for theirs is the kingdom of heaven.
Blessed are those who mourn,
    for they will be comforted.
Blessed are the meek,
    for they will inherit the earth.
Blessed are those who hunger and thirst for righteousness,
    for they will be filled.
Blessed are the merciful,
    for they will be shown mercy.
Blessed are the pure in heart,
    for they will see God.
Blessed are the peacemakers,
    for they will be called sons of God.
Blessed are those who are persecuted because of righteousness,
    for theirs is the kingdom of heaven.
Blessed are you when people insult you, persecute you and falsely say all kinds of evil
    against you because of me. Rejoice and be glad, because great is your reward in
    heaven, for in the same way they persecuted the prophets who were before you.

(Matthew 5:3–12)

What Is a Parable?

When Jesus walked and taught on earth, He had lots of important truths to share about God. Sometimes the easiest way to get across a big idea is to tell a simple story. That is what Jesus did when He told parables. A *parable* is a simple story that teaches a big idea.

In the parable of the lost sheep, Jesus taught how much God loves His children (Matthew 18:10–14; Luke 15:3–7). If one of His children wanders away like a lost sheep, God will search and search until He finds that child. In this famous parable, Jesus calls His children "little ones" (Matthew 18:14).

The parable of the lost sheep is printed below. As you read it, remember that it teaches how much God loves *you*!

Jesus said, "See that you do not look down on one of these little ones. For I tell you that their angels in heaven always see the face of my Father in heaven. What do you think? If a man owns a hundred sheep, and one of them wanders away, will he not leave the ninety-nine on the hills and go to look for the one that wandered off?

"And if he finds it, I tell you the truth, he is happier about that one sheep than about the ninety-nine that did not wander off. In the same way your Father in heaven is not willing that any of these little ones should be lost" (Matthew 18:10–14).

Why Do Some Bibles Have Red Letters?

Some editions of the Bible use red letters for all of Jesus' spoken words. The red letters show the importance of Jesus' words and make them easier for the reader to find.

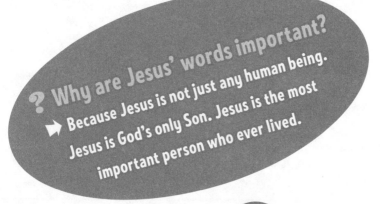

? Why are Jesus' words important?
➤ Because Jesus is not just any human being. Jesus is God's only Son. Jesus is the most important person who ever lived.

Which Bible Is Right for Me?

Some Bibles have colorful pictures and maps. Others have study guides and notes. Some Bibles use literal translations from the original Greek and Hebrew manuscripts. Others use modern language. Some Bibles are bound in leather and trimmed with gold. Others are paperback.

The best way to discover which Bible is right for you is to visit your church library or local family bookstore and look at their selection of Bibles. Hold the Bible in your hands. Open it up. Flip through the pages. Read a few passages. It is important that you have a Bible you can understand. This is because God wants you to understand what the Bible has to say about Him and His Son Jesus. God wants you to understand how much He loves *you*! (Colossians 2:2; 2 Timothy 3:15–17; 1 John 3:1).

If you can't afford to buy a Bible, talk to your pastor, youth minister, or other trusted adult who loves Jesus. Tell him or her that you would very much like to have your own Bible. God wants everyone to have a Bible. And that includes *you*!

Five Helpful Hints for Reading Your Bible:

1. Before you start reading your Bible, take a moment to pray. Ask God to open your mind to understanding His Word (Colossians 1:9).

2. Select a short section of the Bible. Before you start reading, ask yourself, "What kind of book is this?" Remember, the Bible is actually a library of different kinds of books! You also might want to ask, "Why was this book written?" If you don't know the answers to these questions, use a study Bible that gives background information for each book.

3. Read a short section of the Bible carefully. Don't rush. Think about what the words mean.

4. Ask yourself, "What is God trying to say to me right now?"

5. Decide how you want to act on what on what you've learned.

Is It OK to Write in My Bible?

God wants you to remember His words (Proverbs 4:5). In order to remember God's words, some people underline or highlight certain verses of the Bible. Other people make notes in the margins of their Bible. When you remember God's words, you can use them in your day-to-day life.

If your mom and dad say it is OK, then yes, it is all right to write in your Bible.

What's the Point of Memorizing Bible Verses?

When you memorize a Bible verse, you are carrying the Word of God in your head and in your heart. This is a very good and helpful thing. Why? Because if, for example, you are feeling worried, you can remember that God's Word promises, "Be strong and courageous. Do not be terrified; do not be discouraged, for the LORD your God will be with you wherever you go" (Joshua 1:9). Or if you are facing a task that seems impossible, you can remember that God's Word promises, "Everything is possible for him who believes" (Mark 9:23).

Life is full of ups and downs. The Bible says that God's Word is like a light that shines in the dark to show you the way (see Psalm 119:105). The more familiar you are with God's Word, the easier it is for you to hear His loving voice (see Isaiah 30:21).

But what if you're not good at memorizing? Don't worry. Memorizing Bible verses is fun and easy to do. Everyone learns in different ways. Some of us can look at a short Bible verse and remember it right away. Others have to work a little harder. With a little practice, you will find the way that works best for you.

Here are some helpful hints for
memorizing Bible verses

Listen. Listen as a friend reads a Bible verse to you, or make an audiotape of yourself reading the verse and listen to it. Keep listening to it until you have the verse memorized.

Read. Read the Bible verse to yourself over and over until it becomes familiar to you. Read it out loud. Read it silently. When you feel pretty sure that you know the verse, say it out loud by memory.

Touch. Sometimes it is helpful to cover parts of the Bible verse with your hand as you remember them. Do this until you can cover the entire verse with your hand and say it out loud.

Write. Write the Bible verse ten times. At first, you will need to look at the verse as you write it. Eventually, you will be able to write it without looking at the Bible. When you think you have it memorized, say it out loud. Some people like to write favorite Bible verses on note cards and tape them on a spot where they will see them each day, like on the bathroom mirror, or the refrigerator door.

Imagine. When you read the verse, use your imagination to create pictures in your mind that will help you remember the verse.

Memorize with a friend. Working with a friend to memorize Bible verses can be lots of fun. Encourage each other as you use the methods above. Together you can see which methods work best for each of you.

What Is Christianity?

Christianity is a religion based on the life and teachings of Jesus Christ. Christianity began with a few disciples in the small Roman province of Judea more than two thousand years ago. People who believe in and follow Christ are called Christians (Acts 11:26).

The early Christians "devoted themselves to the apostles' teaching and to the fellowship, to the breaking of bread and to prayer. . . . And the Lord added to their number daily those who were being saved" (Acts 2:42, 47). From Judea, Christianity quickly spread throughout the Roman Empire.

Today, Christians live in every nation of the world. More than two billion people, or about one-third of the people on earth, call themselves Christians.

It is estimated that nearly **700 million** Christians are **fifteen** years old or **younger.**

That's a lot of Christian kids!

Why Do Some Christians Carry Signs That Say "John 3:16" at Football Games?

Jesus said, "For God so loved the world that he gave his one and only Son, that whoever believes in him shall not perish but have eternal life" (John 3:16).

John 3:16 is one of the most famous verses in the Bible.

It is famous because in just twenty-six words, it sums up the good news of Christianity. Because it is so short, it is a good Bible verse to put on a sign. It is also a good Bible verse to memorize!

What's the Biggest Difference Between Christianity and Other Religions?

Christianity is not just another religion that teaches *about* God. Christianity is a religion centered on having a personal relationship *with* God. This is possible because Christians believe that God is alive. God is real. God has a special plan for the world and for each person in it.

Most importantly, Christians believe that God loves the world and all the people in it (John 3:16). God loves *you*!

What Is the Apostles' Creed?

The Apostles' Creed dates from the very early days of the Christian church. The word *creed* means "I believe." Knowing what you believe is important.

Belief in God is a very good and powerful thing. Jesus said, "Everything is possible for him who believes" (Mark 9:23).

The Apostles' Creed is the most popular summary of Christian beliefs. Saying the Apostles' Creed helps Christians remember what they believe. To this day, the Apostles' Creed is said by Christians in churches around the world.

HERE IS WHAT IT SAYS:

I believe in God, the Father Almighty,
  creator of heaven and earth
I believe in Jesus Christ, his only Son, our Lord.
He was conceived by the power of the Holy Spirit
  and born of the Virgin Mary.
He suffered under Pontius Pilate,
   was crucified, died, and was buried.
He descended to the dead.*
On the third day he rose again.
He ascended into heaven,
  and is seated at the right hand of the Father.
He will come again to judge the living and the dead.
I believe in the Holy Spirit,
  the holy catholic church,
  the communion of saints,
  the forgiveness of sins,
  the resurrection of the body,
  and the life everlasting. Amen.

*Some churches do not include this line.

What Does the Word *Catholic* Mean in the Apostles' Creed?

The word *catholic* means universal. As it appears in the Apostles' Creed, the "holy catholic church" refers to the universal or worldwide Christian church. The holy catholic church consists of all the believers in Jesus who have ever lived on earth.

When the word *Catholic* is capitalized, it refers to the Roman Catholic Church, which makes up part of the worldwide Christian church and has its headquarters at Vatican City, which is near Rome, Italy.

What Is Faith?

The Bible teaches, "Faith is being sure of what we hope for and certain of what we do not see" (Hebrews 11:1). The word *faith* means to trust and believe with confidence. Faith is a gift from God. Faith is as natural as breathing.

Would you like more faith?

Ask God, and He promises that He will give it to you.

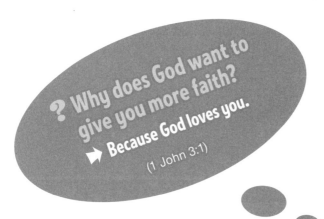

? Why does God want to give you more faith?

➡ Because God loves you.

(1 John 3:1)

What Is Sin?

God is perfect. Human beings are not.

Sin is the imperfect condition of the human body, mind, and soul. It is our human nature. It is the way we are born. Human beings make mistakes. Human beings forget how to love. Sometimes human beings are selfish. Sometimes they do bad things on purpose. Sin is what separates us from God. Sin is why we need Jesus to be our Savior.

Sins are unloving thoughts or behaviors.

When a person thinks, *She is so stupid*, or, *He's such a jerk,* those are sinful thoughts. When a person cheats on a test or gossips about a friend, those are sinful behaviors.

Everyone is born with a sinful human nature. Everyone has sinful thoughts and behaviors (Romans 3:23). It's all part of being human. In all of human history there was only one person born without a sinful human nature. That person is Jesus (Hebrews 4:15; 1 Peter 2:22).

Does God Stop Loving Me
When I Sin?

The Bible teaches that sin is what breaks our relationship with God. This is because God is holy (Psalm 99:9).

Human beings are not holy. But because God loves us, He made a way for our sins to be forgiven. The word *forgive* means to excuse or pardon. The Bible says that when God forgives our sins, He also *forgets* them (Jeremiah 31:34)!

God loves us so much, He sent Jesus to earth to die for our sins (John 3:16; Romans 5:8). Because our sins are forgiven through Jesus, we can be friends with God.

When you sin, you make God **very sad.** But God **never stops** loving you, even when you **sin.**

Why Do I Still Sin, Even When I Don't Want To?

Everyone makes mistakes. It's part of being human.

The apostle Paul struggled mightily with sin. "I do not understand what I do," he wrote. "For what I want to do I do not do, but what I hate I do. . . . I have the desire to do what is good, but I cannot carry it out" (Romans 7:15, 18).

When you give in to temptation and sin, you feel bad. Your conscience bothers you. You feel a little bit of shame or guilt. This is OK. Sometimes painful feelings are God's way of protecting you! Just as physical pain warns you of danger to your body, emotional pain warns you of danger to your soul.

So when you sin and feel a pang of guilt, what should you do?

The apostle John wrote, "If we confess our sins, he will forgive our sins, because we can trust God to do what is right. He will cleanse us from all the wrongs we have done" (1 John 1:9 NCV).

Talk to God. Confess your sin. Tell Him you're sorry. Tell Him you want to do better. Ask God to help you. Because Jesus died for your sins, God promises that He will forgive you. No matter what.

God's **love for you** is **bigger** than any sin.

Why Did Christians Invent Hospitals and Orphanages?

Jesus came to earth to teach and show us what God is like. Jesus taught that God loves everyone. Jesus showed God's love by helping, healing, and welcoming everyone He met. This was a new idea. Back in Jesus' day, people who were sick and poor were left alone to care for themselves. There were no hospitals. There were no children's homes for orphans.

To show us what God is like, Jesus put His love into action. When Jesus saw hungry people, He fed them. When Jesus saw sick people, He healed them. He encouraged people who were lonely. He welcomed people who didn't have friends.

To explain why people should help each other, Jesus told His disciples about people who visited people in prison and helped total strangers who were hungry, thirsty, sick, and in need of clothes.

"I tell you the truth," said Jesus, "whatever you did for one of the least of these brothers of mine, you did for me" (Matthew 25:31–40).

Christians in the early church took Jesus' teachings to heart. They made a special effort to take care of orphans, widows, and older people. They visited people in prison. Over time, Christians invented hospitals to take care of sick people.

Christians invented orphanages to take care of children without parents. Christians developed nursing and retirement homes for older people and programs to help people in prison. Christians also developed many organizations to help hungry and hurting people around the world.

When we help other people, we are actually helping Jesus!

Through Jesus, we are all connected.
That is why we need to love and help each other.

What Can I Do to Help People in Need?

Jesus said, "From everyone who has been given much, much will be demanded; and from the one who has been entrusted with much, much more will be asked" (Luke 12:48).

Our life on earth is a gift from God. God wants us to care about people in need.

Once we care, God asks us do to something more. He asks us to use our lives to reach out and help. This is called putting our Christian faith into action.

What are some things you can do to help people in need?

You can pray.

You can visit an older person who is lonely.

You can listen to your friend who is in trouble or sad.

You can write an encouraging letter to a soldier far away from home.

Talk to your mom and dad or your pastor or youth minister.
They will have lots of good ideas too!

Why Is Taking Care of Our Planet Important to Christians?

The Bible teaches that God created our planet, Earth. He created the heavens and the oceans. He created the plants and the fish. He created the birds and the animals. Finally, He created His children, human beings. "God saw all that he had made, and it was very good" (Genesis 1:31).

God loves the world (John 3:16). God loves His children (1 John 3:1). The Bible says God made everything in the world for His children. He gives us water to drink. He gives us wheat to make bread. He gives us delicious fruits and vegetables. He gives us chickens and eggs, fish and cattle. He gives us trees to build houses. He gives us oil to run our factories and cars. What a generous Father God we have! He gives us everything we need.

God told humans to take care of His creation (Genesis 1:26; 2:15). The word for taking care of the earth is called Christian stewardship. The word *stewardship* means to care for another's property.

Our beautiful planet does not belong to us. We did not make it. It belongs to our Father God. Our job as Christians is to take good care of it. Christians believe it is important to keep our air and water clean. It is important to be careful with natural resources like trees and oil. It is important not to litter.

❓ Why do we take good care of our planet?

➡ Taking care of the earth shows God that we do not take His generous gifts for granted.

Taking care of our beautiful planet is one way of saying thank you to God.

Why Do Some Christians Put Fish-Shaped Symbols on Their Cars?

In the early days of the church, Christians were persecuted by the government. They had to meet in secret. Because of the constant danger they faced, the early Christians developed secret signs to identify each other.

One secret sign was the fish. To use the sign, a Christian would draw a simple curve-shaped line of half a fish on the wall or in the dirt. A non-Christian passing by would think nothing of this. But another Christian knew what to do and completed the sign by drawing the other half of the fish! The secret sign of the fish encouraged Christians. It helped them feel not so alone.

The fish was also a symbol that reminded the early Christians of what they believed. Why a fish? Jesus' first disciples, Peter and his brother Andrew were fishermen. When Jesus saw them casting their nets, He said, "Come, follow me, and I will make you fishers of men" (Mark 1:17).

Two thousand years later, the symbol of the fish is still being used by millions of Christians around the world. Isn't that amazing?

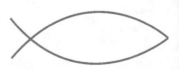

Is There a Way to Tell Christians Apart from Other People?

Jesus said, "All men will know that you are my disciples, if you love one another" (John 13:35).

Loving other people is not always easy.

But this is what Christians try to do.

? Why do Christians try to love other people?

➡️ **Because God is love.**

(1 John 4:8)

What Is Prayer?

Prayer is a conversation with God. One part of a conversation is talking. The other part is listening. God created you to enjoy a personal relationship with Him. The more time you spend with God, the better you get to know Him and the more you grow to love Him.

God wants to listen to you.

(Psalm 34:15)

He is interested in all your thoughts and feelings. He is interested in all your friendships, hopes, and dreams. He is interested in everything about you (Psalm 139:1).

God wants to talk to you.

(Isaiah 30:21)

He wants to comfort you when you are feeling sad, lonely, worried, or afraid. He wants to laugh with you when you are happy. He wants to help you when you have a difficult decision to make.

? Why is God so interested in listening and talking to you?

➡ **Because God loves you.**
(1 John 3:1)

Do I Need to Use Special Words When I Pray?

You don't need to use special words when you pray. You don't need to use fancy language. You don't need to memorize prayers. You don't need to recite prayers written by other people. You don't need to write down your thoughts before you pray. You don't even need to speak out loud. It's perfectly all right to have a conversation with God silently. This is because God hears your thoughts.

When you pray, just be yourself. Talk to God as if He is your best friend in the whole world. It is all right to cry when you pray. It is all right to laugh too.

Jesus was so close to God that when He prayed, He called God "Abba," which means daddy or papa (Mark 14:36). Jesus says this is how we should pray to God too.

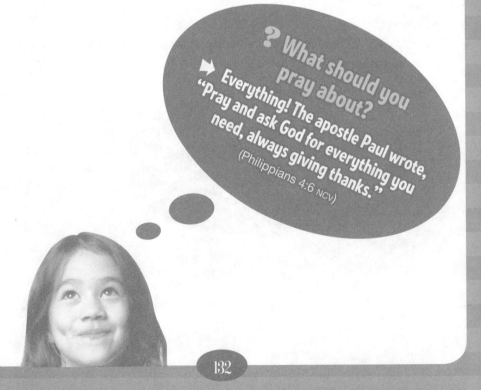

? What should you pray about?

➤ Everything! The apostle Paul wrote, "Pray and ask God for everything you need, always giving thanks." (Philippians 4:6 NCV)

Do I Have to Kneel When I Pray?

You do not have to kneel when you pray. You do not have to close your eyes. You do not have to bow your head. You can pray standing, walking, or sitting. You can pray while you are riding the bus to school. You can pray while you are walking the dog. You can pray while you are lying in your bed at night. If you like, you can pray while you are standing on your head!

Many Christians pray standing up, with their hands held apart, palms up, toward God. Other Christians kneel when they pray. Kneeling is a position that shows you are humble before God. The word *humble* means lowly, or near the ground.

Bowing your head and closing your eyes can help you concentrate.

God does not care what position you are in when you pray.

God just cares that you pray (Romans 12:12; 1 Thessalonians 5:17).

What Is the Lord's Prayer?

When Jesus walked and talked on earth, the disciples noticed that He had a different way of praying. Jesus didn't use fancy language or memorized prayers. He didn't call attention to Himself when He prayed. Often, He slipped away to a quiet place for time alone with His Father God. When Jesus prayed, His words flowed naturally from the bottom of His heart. When Jesus prayed, it was as though He was talking to His best friend in the world.

Jesus' disciples wanted to pray like He did. So they asked, "Lord, teach us to pray" (Luke 11:1). The answer that Jesus gave became known as the Lord's Prayer. It is the most famous prayer in the world. It is repeated by millions of Christians every day around the world.

The Lord's Prayer

Our Father which art in heaven,
Hallowed be thy name.
Thy kingdom come.
Thy will be done,
in earth, as it is in heaven.
Give us this day our daily bread.
And forgive us our debts,
as we forgive our debtors.
And lead us not into temptation,
but deliver us from evil:
For thine is the kingdom, and the power, and the glory,
for ever.
Amen.
(Matthew 6:9–13 KJV)

Why Do We Say "Amen" at the End of Prayers?

The word *amen* means "yes, it is certain" or "so be it." We say "amen" at the end of a prayer to show that what we have said to God is true. We say it to show that we believe that God has heard our prayer. We say it to show that we believe God will answer our prayer (see Psalm 41:13; 1 Corinthians 14:16).

What's the Difference Between "Saying Grace" and "Saying a Blessing" Before Meals?

Grace is a beautiful word. It is used in many ways. The word *grace* means pleasing. To "say grace" is to offer a prayer of thanksgiving before a meal.

Some Christians refer to the mealtime prayer as "saying a blessing." To say a blessing is to ask God to bless the food which one is about to eat. The word *bless* comes from an old English word which means to consecrate, or set apart as holy.

The Bible tells us that Jesus took time to bless the bread before giving it to the disciples to serve five thousand hungry people (Matthew 14:19 KJV, TLB, RSV; Mark 6:41 KJV, RSV; Luke 9:16 KJV, RSV). Other versions of the Bible say that Jesus "gave thanks" before breaking the bread (Matthew 14:19; Mark 6:41 TLB; Luke 9:16 TLB).

Some Christians make up a new prayer each time they eat. Others recite a short memorized prayer. Many Christians like to hold hands when they say grace.

Sometimes we are so hungry it is easy to forget to thank God for our food. But even if you are very hungry, saying grace doesn't have to take a long time.

Here are three short blessings many Christians say before eating:

1 God is great.
God is good.
Let us thank Him
for our food.
Amen.

2 Thank You for the
world so sweet.
Thank You for the
food we eat.
Thank You for the
birds that sing.
Thank You, God,
for everything.
Amen.

3 Bless us, O Lord,
and these your gifts,
which we are about
to receive
from your bounty.
Through Christ our Lord.
Amen.

Is It OK to Say Grace in a Restaurant?

Yes, it is OK to say grace in a restaurant. God is happy to hear from you anytime, anywhere!

When you say grace in a restaurant, remember to be considerate of other people dining around you. The purpose of saying grace is not to draw attention to yourself (Matthew 6:5). The purpose is to simply thank God.

What's a Good Bedtime Prayer?

Bedtime is a great time to talk to God. You can thank Him for the day you just had. You can talk to Him about tomorrow. You can ask God to be with you in your dreams. You can ask God to send His angels to watch over you while you sleep (see Psalm 91:11).

Sometimes it is nice to say a short prayer with your mom or dad before you go to sleep.

Here is a popular bedtime prayer for children:

Now I lay me down to sleep.
I pray the Lord my soul to keep.
Let Thy love guide me through the night.
And wake me with Thy morning light.
God bless Mom and Dad and . . .
(Here you can have fun listing everyone
in the whole world you care about!)
I pray all these things in Jesus' name.
Amen.

Can I Know for Sure That God Hears My Prayers?

Yes, you can know for sure that God hears you when you pray. You can also know that God sees you when you pray.

How can you know this? The Bible promises, "The LORD sees the good people and listens to their prayers" (Psalm 34:15 NCV).

God's Word also promises, "How gracious [God] will be when you cry for help! As soon as he hears, he will answer you" (Isaiah 30:19). The apostle John wrote, "This is the confidence we have in approaching God: that if we ask anything according to his will, he hears us" (1 John 5:14).

God promises that He hears and sees you when you pray.

You can trust God about this, because He always keeps His promises (Deuteronomy 7:9; 1 Corinthians 1:9).

Can I Know for Sure That God Will Answer My Prayers?

Yes, you can know for sure that God will answer your prayers.

Jesus promised, "Whatever you ask for in prayer, believe that you have received it, and it will be yours" (Mark 11:24). Jesus also promised, "Ask and it will be given to you; seek and you will find; knock and the door will be opened to you" (Matthew 7:7).

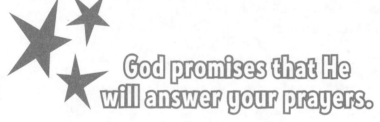

God promises that He will answer your prayers.

Sometimes God's answers are not what we want to hear. Sometimes He answers no or wait. God may not always give you what you want. But you can trust that God will always give you what you need. This is because God loves you and knows what's best for you. God always gives you the perfect answer to your prayer.

Can God Actually Talk to Me?

Yes, God can actually talk to you. The secret is to learn how to hear His voice. Sometimes that means taking time to be quiet and listen.

This is not always easy to do. It is easy to be distracted by the TV. Or the sound of cars going by. Or the smell of dinner cooking. Sometimes it is easy to be distracted by the noise of your own thoughts! It is easy to let your mind wander. Instead of listening for God, you find yourself thinking of a cool glass of milk and fresh-baked chocolate-chip cookies . . . Yum!

But wait. Back to learning how to hear God's voice!

God's voice is different from our thoughts. God says things you never would think of yourself. God's voice is a gentle whisper (1 Kings 19:12). Sometimes God speaks a Bible verse. Sometimes He speaks through the words in a book or sermon. Many times God speaks through people we love. Sometimes God speaks a tender word of comfort. Sometimes He speaks a stern word of wisdom. God always knows exactly what you need to hear (Isaiah 30:21). Take time to listen to God.

? Why is God so eager to talk to you?
➔ Because God loves you.
(1 John 3:1)

Is It OK to Pray for Help on a Test?

Yes, it is OK to pray for help on a test. But prayer is not an excuse for not being prepared! Prayer is not a magic wand. God expects you to do your homework and study for tests. That is your responsibility.

On the day of a test, you might pray, "God, You know how hard I've studied for this test. Please help me not be nervous. Help me remember everything I can and do my best. Thank You for caring so much. I love You. In Jesus' name, amen."

If you have not done your homework or studied as you should, ask God to forgive you. And ask Him to help you be better prepared next time!

God wants to help you do well in school.

God wants the best for you in all things (Jeremiah 29:11)!

What Does It Mean to Pray "in Jesus' Name"?

Many Christians close their prayers with the words, "In Jesus' name, amen." This is because Jesus said to the disciples, "I will do whatever you ask in my name, so that the Son may bring glory to the Father. You may ask me for anything in my name, and I will do it" (John 14:13–14).

Saying the words "In Jesus' name" at the end of a prayer is not like a magic formula. It does not guarantee that God will answer your prayer exactly the way you want. When you pray to the Father "in Jesus' name," it is a way of telling God you know His Son, Jesus. You love Jesus. You trust Jesus. When you pray to the Father in Jesus' name, it is a way of saying, "Whatever You think is best for me, God. Not my will, but Your perfect will be done."

It is not necessary to end every prayer with the words, "In Jesus' name." This is because God does not care about the exact words you use when you pray. God does care that you mean what you say.

When you pray, God wants you to speak to Him sincerely, from the bottom of your heart. Why is this? Because God loves you (1 John 3:1).

Is It OK to Pray Out Loud with Another Person?

Yes, it is OK to pray out loud with another person. In fact, you can pray with as many people as you like! This is because there is special power when you pray with other people.

Jesus said, "If two of you on earth agree about anything you ask for, it will be done for you by my Father in heaven. For where two or three come together in my name, there am I with them" (Matthew 18:19–20).

The next time you are with friends, you might want to try praying together. See what an exciting experience praying with friends can be!

Ten Tips for Praying Out Loud with Friends:

1. You might sit or stand in a circle — whatever is comfortable.

2. You might hold hands.

3. Close your eyes.

4. Ask God's Holy Spirit to be with you to help guide your thoughts and prayers.

5. You don't have to pray in any special order.

6. Expect times of silence. Don't feel that you need to break the silence.

7. Listen for God's Holy Spirit during times of silence. He might give you ideas about what to pray.

8. Jesus promises that He is with you when you pray (Matthew 18:19–20). See if you can feel His presence.

9. When you feel that everyone has had their turn speaking, listen to the silence one last time.

10. You might close by saying the Lord's Prayer together.

Is It OK to Pray with a Friend over the Phone?

Yes, it is OK to pray with a friend over the phone. It is also OK to pray with a friend over the computer. God hears your prayers, no matter where you say them.

God hears your unspoken prayers too.

God is such a good listener that He knows what you need even before you ask Him (Matthew 6:8)!

? Why is God such a good listener?
➤ Because God loves you.
(1 John 3:1)

What Is a Prayer Journal?

A prayer journal is like a diary between you and God. It provides a written record of your prayers.

If you decide to keep a prayer journal, it doesn't need to be fancy. It can be as simple as a spiral notebook. Some people write in a prayer journal every day. Others write in it once or twice a week. Whatever works for you is fine. God is always happy to hear from you.

When you write in your prayer journal, be sure to put the date at the top of the page. That way, as weeks go by, you can go back and see how God has worked in your life. When you are feeling low, reading through your prayer journal can help you remember how God has helped you in the past (Deuteronomy 8:2; Psalms 77:11; 78:35; 105:5; 143:5; Isaiah 46:9; Matthew 16:9–10).

Should you choose to keep a prayer journal, you will be amazed to see how God answers your prayers!

What Should I Do When I Can't Think of What to Pray?

There's no way you *have* to pray, but one easy way to remember how to pray can be found in the word ACTS. In the Bible, the book of Acts tells the story of the early church. Like Christians today, the early Christians prayed a lot (Acts 1:13–14)!

The ACTS way of praying works well for all kinds of prayer. You can use the ACTS way of praying when you pray out loud. You can use it when you pray silently. You can use it when you pray by writing in your prayer journal.

The ACTS Way to Pray

A **Adoration.** Start your prayer time by praising God. Tell God how wonderful He is. Tell God how much you appreciate His love.

C **Confession.** Confess to God all the ways you've let Him down. Tell God you are sorry for your sins. Ask for His forgiveness.

T **Thanksgiving.** Thank God for all the good things in your life. Once you get started, this may take longer than you think! No matter what your troubles are, there is always much to be thankful for.

S **Supplication.** The word *supplication* means to humbly and earnestly ask. Tell God what's going on in your life. Share your prayer requests. Don't hold back. Tell God everything, from the bottom of your heart. God loves you, and He wants to hear every detail.

What Is Intercessory Prayer?

Intercessory is a big word that means to ask on another's behalf. Intercessory prayer is praying for another person.

Say you have a friend who is very sick—so sick he can't pray for himself. When you pray for that friend, you are asking God for healing on his behalf. To pray for another person is a very loving thing to do. It is also good for you.

The apostle Paul wrote, "Do not worry about anything, but pray and ask God for everything you need" (Philippians 4:6 NCV).

When someone you love is in trouble, God doesn't want you to worry.

God wants you to pray (1 Peter 5:7)!

Is It True That When Jesus Was on Earth, He Prayed for Me?

Yes, it is true that when Jesus was on earth, He prayed for you.

Before Jesus died, He had a big conversation with His Father God. First, He prayed for Himself. Then He prayed for His disciples. And then He prayed for all the believers in the world—including believers who hadn't been born yet! He prayed for *you*. Isn't that amazing?

After Jesus prayed for His disciples, He said, "I pray also for those who will believe in me through their message, that all of them may be one, Father, just as you are in me and I am in you. May they also be in us so that the world may believe that you have sent me. I have given them the glory that you gave me, that they may be one as we are one: I in them and you in me. May they be brought to complete unity to let the world know that you sent me and have loved them even as you have loved me" (John 17:20–23).

Jesus prayed that you will know and love God like He does. Jesus prayed that others will love and believe in Him because of you. Jesus prayed that you will love and enjoy being with other Christians.

? Why did Jesus pray all these things just for you?

➡ **Because He loves you.**
(John 15:9, 13)

Do Miracles Still Happen Today?

Yes, miracles still happen today! Miracles are God's way of showing how much He loves us. Sometimes miracles help people believe in God and Jesus.

The word *miracle* means wonderful.

Miracles are not magic tricks. They are things God does that are above the laws of nature. Miracles are real, and miracles still happen.

The same power that God gave to Jesus to help and heal people is available to Christians today. Jesus was very clear about this when He said, "Anyone who has faith in me will do what I have been doing. He will do even greater things than these, because I am going to the Father. And I will do whatever you ask in my name, so that the Son may bring glory to the Father. You may ask me for anything in my name, and I will do it" (John 14:12–14).

Sometimes, when a prayer is answered with a miracle, it is easy to say, "Oh, that was just a coincidence" or, "I was just lucky." But God is bigger than coincidences or luck. God is like the glue that holds everything in our lives together (see Colossians 1:17).

Miracles happen every day.

They are one way God shows that He loves you.

The Church

What Is the Church?

The worldwide church is made up of all the Christians on earth. The church is the living body of Jesus Christ at work in the world today (1 Corinthians 12:27; Ephesians 1:22–23).

The **church** is a living example of **God's love** for the world. The church gives us **glimpses** of God's kingdom on earth.

(Luke 4:43; 10:9)

Why Is the Church Called the "Body of Christ"?

Now you are the body of Christ, and each one of you is a part of it," the apostle Paul wrote to members of the early church (1 Corinthians 12:27). Paul also wrote, "And God placed all things under his feet and appointed him to be head over everything for the church, which is his body" (Ephesians 1:22–23).

Through God's Holy Spirit, Jesus lives in the hearts of Christians around the world.

Jesus uses the hearts and minds and bodies of Christians to get God's work done on earth. He uses our minds to think of ways to put God's love into action. He uses our feet to carry us to people who are lonely or sick or sad. He uses our arms to wrap around people who need a hug. He uses our mouths to speak kind and encouraging words, and to tell others about God.

? Why does Jesus use Christians this way?

➡ **To show the world God's love.**
(John 3:16)

Does a Church Have to Have a Building?

The word *church* has come to mean a building where Christians meet. But a church does not need a building. A church is made up of people who love Jesus. A church is any group of Christians who meet together regularly to pray and worship God (Acts 2:42; 12:5).

A church is a community of people who believe in Jesus (Acts 9:31; 16:5). Some churches are very small and meet in peoples' homes (Romans 16:5; Philemon 2). Other churches are very large and meet in huge auditoriums. Some churches have their own buildings. Other churches rent space in schools and gymnasiums.

In God's eyes, the building is the least important part of any church. This is because God doesn't love buildings.

God loves people.

Why Does God Want Me to Be Involved in a Church?

There is an old saying that there are no "Lone Ranger" Christians. This is because God did not create you to be alone. The church is God's great big family, and He wants you to be part of it (Galatians 6:10; 1 Timothy 3:15)!

God wants you to share His love with others (John 13:35; Ephesians 5:2).

God wants your faith to grow (2 Thessalonians 1:3). Being involved in a church is a great way to do these things.

God wants **you** to be **involved** in a church so you can:

Learn more about God.

Pray with other Christians.

Worship God with other Christians.

Reach out and help other people in need.

Have fun with friends!

Why Are There So Many Different Kinds of Churches?

No two churches are exactly alike, because no two people are exactly alike. There are many different kinds of churches, because there are many different kinds of Christians.

Some churches have services only on Sunday. Other churches have services every day of the week. Some churches own their own building. Other churches meet in homes.

Some churches celebrate Communion once a month. Other churches celebrate Communion every Sunday. Some churches baptize babies by sprinkling them with water. Other churches baptize children and grown-ups in waist-deep pools of water.

Some churches have choirs and sing traditional hymns. Other churches have worship teams with electric guitars and sing modern praise songs. Some churches use a prayer book. Other churches use an overhead projector.

? What do all these churches have in common?

➡ **They are all made up of people who love Jesus.**
(Acts 2:42, 46-47)

Is It OK for Me to Invite a Friend to Visit My Church?

To invite a friend to church is a very loving and generous thing to do. When you invite a friend to church, you are sharing your love for Jesus. This makes God very happy!

God's church is like a beautiful lamp shining in the darkness. Jesus said, "No one lights a lamp and hides it in a jar or puts it under a bed. Instead, he puts it on a stand, so that those who come in can see the light" (Luke 8:16).

Before you invite a friend to church, be sure to ask your mom and dad.

What Is Baptism?

In Jesus' day, people who wanted to turn away from their sins and toward God were baptized. They waded into a river where a prophet named John the Baptist dipped them in the water and said a prayer. The word *baptize* means to dip. Water symbolizes the washing away of sins.

Baptism was very important to Jesus. Jesus was baptized when He was thirty years old. His baptism marked the beginning of His ministry on earth (Matthew 3:13–17; Mark 1:9–11; Luke 3:21–23). Because Jesus was God's Son, He didn't have to turn away from sin. At the same time, because He was human, Jesus did experience temptation (Matthew 4:1–11; Mark 1:12–13; Luke 4:1–13). Jesus was baptized out of loving obedience to His Father God, and to set an example for us to follow.

Before ascending into heaven, Jesus told His disciples, "Go and make disciples of all nations, baptizing them in the name of the Father and of the Son and of the Holy Spirit" (Matthew 28:19; see also Mark 16:15–16). The disciples loved Jesus and obeyed. From the very earliest days of the church, believers were baptized (Acts 2:41).

Christian churches around the world have many different ways of doing baptisms. Some churches baptize babies and very young children. Other churches require that children be old enough to make their own decision to be baptized. Sometimes adults are baptized. You are never too old to be baptized!

Some churches sprinkle or pour water over the head of the person being baptized. Other churches have special indoor pools deep enough for a grown-up to be totally immersed in water. Christians around the world are also baptized in rivers, ponds, oceans, and swimming pools!

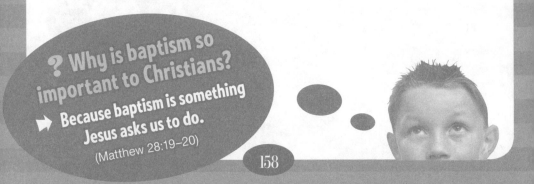

? Why is baptism so important to Christians?

➡ Because baptism is something Jesus asks us to do.
(Matthew 28:19–20)

158

What Is Communion?

On the night before His death, Jesus gathered with the disciples for their last meal together.

The apostle Paul wrote, "The Lord Jesus, on the night he was betrayed, took bread, and when he had given thanks, he broke it and said, 'This is my body, which is for you; do this in remembrance of me.' In the same way, after supper he took the cup, saying, 'This cup is the new covenant in my blood; do this, whenever you drink it, in remembrance of me'" (1 Corinthians 11:23–25).

From the very earliest days of the church, believers gathered to break bread and pray together (Acts 2:42; 20:7). When they did this, they remembered Jesus. They also felt His love and presence in a very real and special way.

Communion is the central act of worship in many Christian churches around the world. The word *communion* means to participate together.

Some churches celebrate Communion at every service. Other churches celebrate Communion once a month or twice a year. Some churches use wine. Other churches use grape juice. Some churches use homemade loaves of unleavened bread. Other churches use prepackaged wafers.

Different churches have different names for Communion. Some call it the Great Thanksgiving or Holy Eucharist. Others call it the Lord's Supper, the Mass, the Divine Liturgy, or the Breaking of Bread.

When Christians celebrate Communion, the wine or grape juice is a symbol of Jesus' blood, which He shed for our sins when He suffered on the cross. The bread is a symbol of Jesus' body, which He gave up for our sins when He died on the cross. Through faith, the bread and wine become something more. They help our faith in Jesus grow.

? Why is Communion so important to Christians?

➤ Because Communion is something Jesus asks us to do.

159

Why Do We Sing
Hymns in Church?

Singing is a way to praise God. When we sing, we praise God with words and song. The word *hymn* means song of praise.

Singing is an important part of worship in almost all Christian churches. Thousands of years ago, King David and King Solomon wrote and sang songs of praise to God, which can be found in the book of Psalms. Jesus and the disciples sang hymns together (Matthew 26:30; Mark 14:26). The apostle Paul encouraged members of the early church to "Speak to one another with psalms, hymns and spiritual songs," and to "Sing and make music in your heart to the Lord" (Ephesians 5:19; see also Colossians 3:16).

Singing makes your heart glad. God often speaks to His children through music and the words of hymns.

For example, "Jesus Loves Me" is one of the best-loved children's hymns in the world. The words and tune are simple. But the message has the power to change the world. Can you sing this song?

Jesus loves me! This I know,
For the Bible tells me so;
Little ones to Him belong,
They are weak, but He is strong.
Yes, Jesus loves me!
Yes, Jesus loves me!
Yes, Jesus loves me!

The Bible tells me so.

What's the Difference Between a Pastor, Priest, and Minister ?

Leaders of different churches are called by different names. But their jobs are very similar.

Pastors, priests, and ministers are responsible for the spiritual well-being of their congregations (Ephesians 4:11–13). They work very hard! They teach about the Bible. They deliver helpful sermons. They counsel people in trouble. They organize the activities of the church. They celebrate baptisms and Communion. They marry people and bury people. They pray for all their church members and for the world.

The word *pastor* comes from a word that means shepherd.

A pastor, like a shepherd, watches over his or her "flock," or the people in the church. The word *priest* comes from a word that means superintendent, or person in charge. The word *minister* comes from a word that means servant.

? What do Christian pastors, priests, and ministers have in common?
➡ **They love Jesus.**

Is it True to Be a Missionary, You Have to Travel Far from Home?

Jesus commanded His followers, "Go into all the world and preach the good news to all creation" (Mark 16:15). Over the years, this powerful command has become known as the Great Commission. The word *commission* means authority that is given to someone. Jesus' last words on earth granted authority to the disciples to go out and tell the whole world about God's love.

A Christian missionary is a person who shares the love of Jesus with others. The word *missionary* means one who is sent off. Some missionaries travel to far parts of the world to share the love of Jesus. Other missionaries work close to home. Some missionaries work deep in the jungle. Other missionaries work in the world's biggest cities. Some missionaries teach villagers how to plant crops and dig wells for fresh water. Other missionaries build schools and hospitals. Some missionaries work with adults. Other missionaries work with teenagers and children.

Everyone who loves Jesus is a missionary. This is because wherever you are, you can share the love of Jesus with others. You can share the love of Jesus at home with your family. You can share the love of Jesus with your relatives. You can share the love of Jesus with your friends at school.

You are a missionary!

What Happens When
Someone Is Converted to Christianity?

The word *convert* means to turn around. When you are converted from unbelief to belief in Jesus, your whole life is turned around!

One of the most famous conversion stories is that of the apostle Paul. Paul was first called *Saul*, which means "called by God." Saul was a Jewish religious leader. He was very faithful, smart, and educated. Saul loved God. But because Saul didn't understand how Jesus could be God's Son, he hated Christians.

Saul persecuted people who followed Jesus. The word *persecute* means to follow or chase in order to hurt someone. Going from house to house, Saul chased the Christians and threw them in prison. Because of Paul, many Christians were killed (Acts 22:3–4). Saul's goal was to destroy the church (Acts 8:3)! When Saul learned that there were Christians in a town called Damascus, he could hardly wait to arrest them.

As Saul neared Damascus on his journey, suddenly a light from heaven flashed around him. He fell to the ground and heard a voice say, "Saul, Saul, why do you persecute me?" "Who are you, Lord?" Saul asked. "I am Jesus, whom you are persecuting," he replied. "Now get up and go into the city, and you will be told what you must do" (Acts 9:3–6).

For three days, Saul could not see or eat or drink. He was stunned by having met the resurrected Jesus. Saul was overwhelmed by Jesus' love for him. His life was totally turned around. Now Saul's heart was filled with God's Holy Spirit, and he believed that Jesus was God. He loved Jesus. He loved other Christians. He devoted his life to sharing the good news of Jesus' love with everyone he met.

Saul's life was so turned around that he changed his Jewish name to the Greek name *Paul,* which means "little," or "less." Because he had persecuted Christians, Paul said he was the littlest or "least of all the apostles" (1 Corinthians 15:9; Ephesians 3:8). Paul's Greek name also helped him share the good news of Jesus with people who were not Jewish.

Paul is famous for his missionary journeys and for the letters he wrote to the early church. You can still read his letters today in the New Testament. Paul understood that believing in Jesus makes all the difference in a person's life.

To convert from unbelief to belief in Jesus is a very good thing!

What Does It Mean to Be Born Again?

To be born again is another way of saying to be converted from unbelief to belief in Jesus. The phrase comes from a famous conversation Jesus had with a Jewish religious leader named Nicodemus.

One night Nicodemus came to Jesus and said, "We know you are a teacher from God. For no one could perform the miracles you are doing if God were not with him."

Jesus replied, "I tell you the truth, unless a man is born again, he cannot see the kingdom of God."

"How can a man be born when he is old?" Nicodemus asked. "Surely he cannot enter a second time into his mother's womb to be born!"

Jesus answered, "I tell you the truth, unless a man is born of water and the Spirit he cannot enter the kingdom of God" (see John 3:2–6).

When you **convert** from **unbelief** to **belief** in Jesus, you receive a **brand-new** life. You are **spiritually** **born again.**

Help! What Should I Do When I Think a Church Service Is Boring?

Everyone gets a little sleepy or bored during a church service sometimes. It's not always easy to sit still indoors when outside the sun is shining. It's not always easy to stay awake if you stayed up late the night before. It's not always easy to pay attention, if the preacher is talking about something that is difficult to understand.

Here are a few ideas to help you the next time you find yourself a little bit sleepy or bored:

Tell God how you feel, and ask Him to help you.

Make a list of all the things you are thankful for.

Make a list of nice things you might do for other people.

Read the Bible. (Genesis, the first book in the Bible, is a good place to start!)

Pray for all the people you love.

Close your eyes and see if you can hear God whisper to you in your heart (1 Kings 19:12).

When you ask Him, God will lead your thoughts to Him!

Christian Seasons & Holidays

Why Do We Mark the Passage of Time with BC and AD?

God is eternal. The word *eternal* means forever or endless. Because God is eternal, He lives outside time and space. Although human beings experience time, God in heaven does not. The Bible says that for God "a day is like a thousand years, and a thousand years are like a day" (2 Peter 3:8).

But God loves us so much that He came crashing into human time and space in the form of Jesus, His Son. Jesus' coming to earth is the most important event that has ever happened in human history. The arrival of Jesus on earth is so important that we mark the passage of years in a way that honors and remembers it.

BC stands for Before Christ. AD stands for the Latin phrase *anno Domini*, which means in the year of our Lord."

BC and AD serve as reminders of God's great love for us in Jesus.

Why Do Christians Observe Special Seasons and Holidays?

Time is God's gift to us. Christians celebrate special seasons and holidays as a way of remembering and thanking God throughout the year. The word *holiday* means holy day.

Many Jewish holy days and feasts are described in the Old Testament (Leviticus 23:1–44). The major Christian seasons and holidays, such as Easter and Christmas, focus on the life and teachings of Jesus.

What Is Advent?

Advent is the season that marks the beginning of the Christian church year. Advent begins four Sundays before Christmas and ends on Christmas Eve. The word *advent* means coming or arrival.

Advent is a time when Christians remember that God sent Jesus to earth as a human baby (Matthew 1:18–24; Luke 2:1–20). Advent is a time when Christians prepare their hearts for Christmas and remember God's great love.

What Is an Advent Wreath?

To celebrate the season of Advent, some Christians make a tabletop wreath of evergreens with five candles. Since ancient times, holiday wreaths have been made by twisting evergreen branches into a circular shape.

Because it has no beginning and no end, the circle is a symbol of eternity. The color green is a symbol of God's everlasting life. Candles offer comfort and warmth during the darkest time of year. Candlelight is a symbol of Jesus' victory over the darkness of evil. It is also a symbol of Jesus' love, which shines in our hearts (Romans 5:5).

The Advent wreath has four candles on the outside, three purple and one pink, and a white in the middle.

The three purple candles symbolize hope, peace, and love. They are lit on the first, second, and fourth Sundays of Advent. The pink candle symbolizes joy. It is lit on the third Sunday of Advent. The fifth candle is white and stands tall in the middle of the Advent wreath. The fifth candle symbolizes Jesus. It is lit on Christmas Day. It is like a birthday candle for Jesus!

Is December 25 Really Jesus' Birthday?

No one knows for sure the exact day Jesus was born. The decision to celebrate the birth of Jesus in December was made during the reign of the Roman emperor Constantine the Great (AD 306–337). Constantine was Rome's first Christian emperor.

Life in ancient Roman times was not easy. People were superstitious and worshiped many gods, including the sun and Saturn, the god of crops. The dark days of winter were a time of great worry. What if the sun never returned? Who would shine upon their fields and vineyards? Each year the Romans eagerly looked forward to the winter solstice on December 21, when the sun returned and the days grew longer.

For one week, beginning on December 17, the ancient Romans celebrated with a festival called Saturnalia. They sang and danced and feasted. They decorated trees, a symbol of growth, with bits of shiny metal, and they gave gifts to each other. They celebrated the return of light to a dark world.

The emperor Constantine loved Jesus. In many ways Jesus was like the sun. Jesus brought spiritual light into a dark world. Jesus warmed peoples' cold hearts. Jesus helped people shine with His love. Constantine decided that no longer would Romans worship Saturn and the sun god. Instead, the Romans would worship God's Son.

The first mention of December 25 as the birth date of Jesus was noted in AD 336 in an early Roman calendar. The word *Christmas* comes from an early English phrase that means "Mass of Christ."

Today most Christians celebrate Christmas on December 25. Because Eastern Orthodox Christians use a different calendar, they celebrate Christmas on January 7.

For Christians around the world, Christmas is a happy, joyful season. It is a time of feasting, singing, and gift giving. It is a time to celebrate God's love for us.

Why Do We Give Gifts at Christmas?

Giving gifts at Christmas is a loving thing to do. Receiving gifts is fun too! But sometimes we can get so excited about Christmas presents that we almost forget the reason we are giving and receiving them.

The Bible says that God loves to give good gifts to His children (Matthew 7:11). We give gifts at Christmas to remind us of God's greatest gift to the world—His Son, Jesus. We give gifts at Christmas to remember and celebrate God's great generosity and love (John 3:16; Romans 6:23; 2 Corinthians 9:15; Ephesians 2:8; 3:7; 1 John 3:1).

Why Do Some People Spell Christmas "Xmas"?

The word *Xmas* is sometimes used as a short way of spelling Christmas.

In the days of the early church, Greek was a commonly spoken and written language (John 19:20). Many early Christians were Greek (Acts 11:20; 17:12; 19:10; 1 Corinthians 12:13). The New Testament was originally written in Greek.

In the Greek alphabet, the cross-shaped letter *X*, or chi, is the first letter of the Greek word *Christos*, which means Christ. In the early church, the Greek letter chi was often used as a symbol for Jesus.

Some people today think it is disrespectful to use the word "Xmas." But the early Christians did not think so.

Are Saint Nicholas and Santa Claus the Same Person?

Saint Nicholas was a real person who was born around AD 280 in modern-day Turkey. Nicholas loved Jesus. He was a Christian bishop who was known for his kindness, wisdom, and generosity. He died in AD 343 on December 6, which became known as Saint Nicholas Day.

There is a famous story about how Saint Nicholas gave a gift to a poor man with three daughters. The man loved his daughters very much. But because he didn't have any money, his daughters couldn't get married. (Back then it was the custom for the bride's family to give money to the groom's family.)

Saint Nicholas threw three bags of gold coins through an open window in the man's house. The bags landed in each daughter's stocking, which the girls had hung above the fireplace to dry. How surprised the girls and their father were to find the three bags of gold! Thanks to Saint Nicholas, each of the daughters now had enough money to marry. Over time, the legend of Saint Nicholas as a giver of gifts grew famous around the world.

Saint Nicholas is especially popular in Holland. On December 5, Saint Nicholas Eve, Dutch children put their wooden shoes out by the fireplace. They go to sleep with hopes that Saint Nicholas will visit and fill their shoes with treats.

The American legend of *Santa Claus* has its roots in Saint Nicholas. When English settlers arrived in America, they learned about Saint Nicholas from their Dutch neighbors. The Dutch name for Saint Nicholas is "Sinter Klaas." When excited English-speaking children repeated the name quickly, it came out sounding like "Santa Claus!"

For more than a thousand years, Saint Nicholas was pictured as a tall, thin man. He wore a red robe and rode a white horse. In 1809, American author Washington Irving wrote a story that described Saint Nicholas as plump and bearded. Irving's Saint Nicholas smoked a pipe, and rode a wagon in the sky that was filled with gifts. Over the treetops he flew, dropping gifts into children's stockings hung above the fireplace.

On December 23, 1823, the Troy, New York, *Sentinal* newspaper published a poem called "A Visit from St. Nicholas," written by a man named Clement Clarke Moore. Over the years the poem became very famous and became known as "The Night Before Christmas." In Moore's poem, "Saint Nick" had a round belly, twinkling eyes, and a nose like a cherry. He was dressed all in fur, blackened with soot from the chimney. He drove a miniature sleigh with eight tiny flying reindeer: Dasher, Dancer, Prancer, Vixen, Comet, Cupid, Donner, and Blitzen.

In the 1860s, an American cartoonist named Thomas Nast drew Santa Claus with a fluffy white beard. Nast drew the first picture of Santa Claus in his workshop at the North Pole. He also drew the first picture of Santa Claus going over his list of all the "good" and "bad" boys and girls in the world.

In the 1930s, the Coca-Cola Company drew illustrations of Santa for a series of popular advertisements. He wore a red suit trimmed with white fur, a wide buckled belt, and big black boots.

Americans love the legend of Santa Claus. And why not? Giving gifts is a loving and fun thing to do. But sometimes we can get so excited about Santa Claus, we almost forget about Jesus. It is important to remember that Christmas is the day we celebrate Jesus' birthday. It is important to remember that "Jesus is the reason for the season."

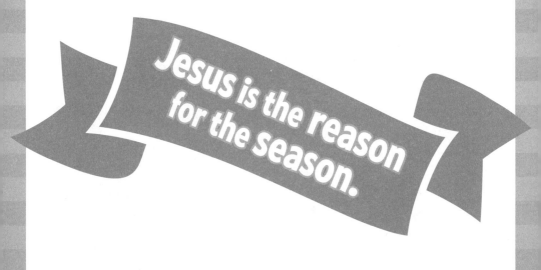

Jesus is the reason for the season.

What Is Lent?

The season of Lent is a period of forty days, not counting Sundays, before Easter Sunday.

Before Jesus began His ministry as a teacher, He spent forty days in the desert. During that time, Jesus fasted and prayed. He grew very close to His Father God. At the end of the forty days, Satan visited Jesus and tried to tempt Him to sin. But Jesus' faith was so strong from His forty days in the desert, He did not sin (Matthew 4:1–11; Mark 1:12–13; Luke 4:1–13).

During the season of Lent, many Christians spend extra time with God. They pray and read the Bible. Sometimes they give something up to help someone else. Maybe they give the money they would otherwise spend on candy bars or video game rentals to help people in need. Or maybe they make a special effort to spend more time with someone who needs a friend.

Lent is a time to grow closer to God. Lent is a time to share God's love with others.

What Is Holy Week?

Holy Week is the final week of Lent and the week before Easter. Holy Week is a time when Christians around the world remember the week leading up to Jesus' death and resurrection.

The two best-known days of Holy Week are Palm Sunday and Good Friday.

Palm Sunday is the first day of Holy Week. Good Friday is the Friday before Easter Sunday. Holy Week is a time to think and pray about God's great love for us (John 3:16; 15:13; Romans 5:8; 1 John 3:16). Holy Week is a time to prepare our hearts for Easter.

Why Do Some People Wave Palm Branches on Palm Sunday?

Palm Sunday is the first day of Holy Week. Palm Sunday is a time when Christians remember when Jesus rode into Jerusalem on a donkey.

On the week before His death, Jesus traveled to Jerusalem to celebrate the Passover meal with His disciples. Crowds of people cast their clothing on the road. They waved palm branches in the air. The palm branches were a symbol of victory and celebration. "Hosanna!" they cried. "Blessed is he who comes in the name of the Lord!" (Matthew 21:1–11; Mark 11:1–11; Luke 19:29–44; John 12:12–19).

The people loved Jesus. Many hoped He was going to be their king on earth. They had no idea that in less than a week, He would die on the cross. They had no idea that three days after he died, He would rise from the dead. All they knew was that they were happy to welcome Him to Jerusalem.

On Palm Sunday, some churches pass out freshly cut palm branches. Some churches also have a parade, where members march up and down the aisle holding their palm branches high. Sometimes the palm branches are woven into the shape of a cross. The palm branches remind us of the day in history when Jesus rode into Jerusalem on a donkey.

Palm Sunday reminds us that even when things don't turn out like we expect, God knows best.

Because God loves us, we can always trust Him no matter what (Deuteronomy 7:9; 1 Corinthians 1:9).

What Does the Word *Hosanna* Mean?

The word *hosanna* or *hosannah*, comes from a Hebrew word which means, "Save us, I pray." It is used to express praise or adoration to God (Matthew 21:9; Mark 11:9; John 12:13).

What Is Good Friday?

Good Friday is the Friday before Easter. It is the day when Christians around the world remember the day Jesus died (Matthew 27:27–66; Mark 15:16–47; Luke 23:26–56; John 19:17–42). Many churches hold special services from noon until three o'clock in the afternoon, to remember the time when Jesus suffered on the cross.

Good Friday is also called Holy Friday or Great Friday.

In Germany, it is called Sorrowful Friday. The Good Friday church service is very somber and quiet. It is a time to pray, and to remember that Jesus loves us so much He was willing to die for us (John 15:9, 13; 1 John 3:16).

At first glance, Good Friday doesn't seem "good" at all. On Good Friday, Jesus suffered and died. But because of Good Friday, there is much good news.

Because of Good Friday, we can thank God for Easter. We can thank God for Jesus' resurrection. We can thank God for forgiving our sins. We can thank God that we will live forever with Him in heaven!

On Good Friday, we can rejoice that nothing, not even death, can separate us from God's love (Romans 8:38–39).

Why Is Easter So Important?

Easter is the most important Christian holy day of the year.

On Easter Sunday, Christians around the world gather to remember and celebrate the fact that Jesus rose from the dead (Matthew 28:1–10; Mark 16:1–8; Luke 24:1–12; John 20:1–18). They celebrate with joyful prayers and singing.

In America, many churches have special sunrise services and meet in the early morning darkness. On hillsides and beaches, they wait for the Easter morning sunrise. As the day dawns, they celebrate the fact that Jesus is not dead but truly alive! The light of the rising sun symbolizes the light of God's risen Son, Jesus.

Because Jesus rose from the dead, the dark power of evil has been broken forever. Because Jesus is alive, and we believe in Him, we will live forever with Him in heaven.

This is very good news!

Why Do We Say "Alleluia!" at Easter?

At Easter, the word *alleluia* is used in many prayers and hymns. The word *alleluia* is a Latin version of the Hebrew word *hallelujah,* which means, "Praise the Lord." So when you say and sing "Alleluia!" at Easter, you are praising the Lord.

Praising the Lord is a good thing to do. God loves it when His children sing His praises—not only on Easter, but every day of the year (Exodus 15:2; Deuteronomy 32:3; Psalms 134:2; 135:3; 146:1; 147:1; Romans 15:4).

Why Do We Celebrate Easter with the Easter Bunny and Painted Eggs?

Easter has long been linked to the season of spring. This is because Easter is a time of celebrating new life and growth. In springtime, the days grow longer. Trees that looked dead during winter grow tender, new leaves. Bulbs that lay buried in the cold, hard earth burst through the soil with colorful, fragrant blossoms. Baby chicks and bunnies are symbols of new life. From the earliest times, the egg has been a symbol of rebirth. To this day, eggs are painted with bright colors and given as gifts.

No one knows for sure how Easter got its name. In the days of the early church, many pagan cultures already observed springtime celebrations and festivals. As believers in Jesus grew in numbers and influence, they attached Christian holidays to existing pagan celebrations. Historians believe that Easter most likely got its name from *Eastre*, the northern European goddess of springtime and fertility, who had a springtime festival of the same name. Or it may have come from the old German word *eostarun*, which means dawn.

Easter is also closely linked with the Jewish celebration of Passover, an eight-day holiday that celebrates the exodus of the Israelites from Egypt. On the night before Jesus died, He celebrated the Passover meal with His disciples (Matthew 26:19–28; Mark 14:12–24; Luke 22:7–20; 1 Corinthians 11:23–25). Passover and Easter are both celebrated in the spring.

The Easter Bunny is a legendary character brought to America by early German settlers. Americans love the Easter Bunny! And why not? Giving and receiving baskets filled with colorful jellybeans and yummy chocolate is fun—and delicious!

But sometimes we can get so excited about the Easter Bunny, we almost forget about Jesus. It is important to remember that Easter celebrates the most important day in human history. Easter celebrates the day Jesus rose from the dead to live forever!

Why Is Easter
Always on a Different Date?

Did you ever wonder why Easter falls on a different date each year? It is because there is an ancient formula for calculating when Easter will take place. Get out your calendar and pencil, and see if you can figure out when Easter will be!

Easter is *the first Sunday after the first full moon that occurs on or after the first day of spring on March 21.* This full moon may happen on any date between March 21 or April 18, including those days. If the full moon falls on a Sunday, Easter is the Sunday following. Easter is always on a Sunday but cannot be earlier than March 22 or later than April 25.

Because Eastern Orthodox Christians use a different method for figuring out the date of Easter, they often celebrate Easter on a different day.

What Is Pentecost?

Pentecost is the name of an ancient Jewish festival that takes place about fifty days after Passover. The word *Pentecost* means fiftieth day.

At the first Pentecost, about ten days after Jesus ascended into heaven, the disciples gathered in Jerusalem. Like the sound of a rushing wind, God's Holy Spirit arrived and filled their hearts. They spoke about God's love in languages they did not know. Their lives were changed forever. Many new people came to believe in Jesus. It was a miracle (Acts 2)! It was also the beginning of the Christian church.

For Christians, Pentecost is celebrated on the seventh Sunday (about fifty days) after Easter. It is a time when Christians celebrate the arrival of the Holy Spirit on earth. It is also a time for celebrating the birth of the Christian church. Some churches celebrate Pentecost with a birthday cake and candles!

"Jesus" in different languages:

CHINESE	耶穌
DUTCH	Jezus
FINNISH	Jeesus
FRENCH	Jésus
ITALIAN	Gesù
JAPANESE	イエス・キリスト
SPANISH	Jesús
SWAHILI	Yesu

What Is All Saints' Day?

All Saints' Day is a Christian holy day that honors all saints, known and unknown.

> The word *saint* means
> **set apart** for God.
> The members of the
> early Christian church
> called one another **"saints."**
>
> (Acts 9:13; Romans 15:25; 2 Corinthians 9:1; 1 Timothy 5:10)

Because you believe in Jesus, *you* are a saint! Happy All Saints' Day to *you* on November 1!

? Who is a saint?
➤ A saint is any person who believes in Jesus.

What Kind of Holiday Is Halloween?

Many years ago, All Saints' Day was known as All Hallows Day. *Hallows* is an old English word that means saints. All Saints' or All Hallows Day is November 1.

The word *Halloween* comes from "All Hallows Eve." Halloween takes place on October 31, the evening before All Saints' or All Hallows Day.

Halloween is not a Christian or church holiday. Halloween began as a Druid celebration called Samhain, or festival of the dead, in northern Europe. The Druids were people who had not yet heard of Jesus. Druids believed that on the eve of November 1, the souls of the dead came and mingled with the living. This was a very scary thought. The Druids carved turnips and potatoes and put candles inside to symbolize ghostly spirits. They built big bonfires and offered sacrifices of crops and animals to cruel spirits. They dressed up in costumes to disguise themselves from evil sprits.

Even after they became Christians, some people in northern Europe continued these customs and called it Halloween. People who came from Ireland brought Halloween to America in the 1840s. American pumpkins made better jack-o'-lanterns than turnips and potatoes!

Over the years, Halloween has become a popular time for parties and trick-or-treating. It is fun to dress up in costumes and go door to door for candy. Sometimes it is fun to be scared. But it is important to remember that Halloween is a holiday that was started by people who did not know God or Jesus. That is why Halloween is dark and scary.

> ## God is NOT dark and scary.
> ## God is light and love.
>
> (John 8:12; 1 John 1:5)

Was There Really a Saint Valentine?

Yes, there once was a Christian named Valentine who lived in Rome. Saint Valentine loved Jesus and refused to worship the Roman gods. Because of his Christian faith, Valentine was thrown in jail and sentenced to death.

While he was in jail, Valentine became friends with many children. The children loved Saint Valentine and passed notes to him through the bars of his jail cell window. Valentine also became friends with the jailer's beautiful daughter.

Valentine was put to death on February 14, 269. Before he died, Valentine wrote the jailer's daughter a loving farewell note. The note was signed "From your Valentine."

Over time, February 14 became known as Saint Valentine's Day. It is a day for exchanging simple expressions of love, such as poems, flowers, cards, and candy. To this day, cards of loving affection are known as "valentines."

Of course, you don't have to wait for Valentine's Day to share your love with someone. God wants us to love each other every day of the year (John 13:34; Romans 12:10)!

Why Do We Celebrate Saint Patrick's Day with Shamrocks?

The man who became known as Saint Patrick was born with the name Maewyn Succat, in Britain, around AD 389. At age sixteen, Maewyn was captured by pirates and sold into slavery in Northern Ireland. In Ireland, Maewyn served as a shepherd for an Irish chieftain. While he watched the sheep, Maewyn prayed and grew close to God. After six years of slavery, he escaped from his captors and fled to Britain.

Maewyn loved Jesus with all his heart. He dreamed of one day returning to Ireland to share God's love with his captors. But he wasn't educated, so Maewyn went to live and study in a monastery in France. The priests at the monastery taught Maewyn how to read and write. Finally, he became a priest and took the Christian name *Patrick*, which means noble.

Over time, Saint Patrick converted many people in Ireland to Christianity. He started more than three hundred churches and baptized more than 120,000 new Christians. According to legend, Saint Patrick used the Irish shamrock, a kind of three-leafed clover, to explain the idea of the Holy Trinity to the Irish.

"How can your God be three persons in one?" the Irish asked.

Saint Patrick plucked a green shamrock from the ground and held it up for all to see. "See these three leaflets?" he asked. "One is for the Father, two is for the Son, three is for the Holy Ghost. Three different leaflets, but all part of the same shamrock. So 'tis with the Holy Trinity."

The day of his death, March 17, became known as Saint Patrick's Day. In Ireland, Saint Patrick's Day is a national, religious holiday. People thank God for Saint Patrick by attending special church services. They wear shamrocks and gather together with family and friends.

In America, Saint Patrick's Day is mostly a nonreligious holiday. People wear green clothing, march in parades, and have parties.

What Is Christian Fellowship?

Christian *fellowship* is spending time with friends who believe in Jesus. Friends who believe in Jesus can share with each other what they know and love about Him. Friends who believe in Jesus can pray with and for each other. Spending time with friends who believe in Jesus is fun!

When friends who believe in Jesus gather together, Jesus promises that He is with them too (Matthew 18:19–20). Isn't that amazing?

Is It True That Christians Can't Have Any Fun?

Some people have the wrong idea about Christianity. They think that it is a religion full of rules about what you can and can't do. They think that Christians can't have any fun.

A funny thing happens when you choose to follow Jesus and His teachings in the Bible. You feel good. You have joy. Did you ever feel so happy that you wanted to burst out singing? Or do a cartwheel? That is how it feels when you follow Jesus. That is how it feels when you know deep in your heart that you are trying your best to please God.

> **To love is to be kind.**
>
> **It is to smile and laugh.**
>
> **It is to think about what is good for other people.**
>
> **It is to enjoy deep and lasting friendships.**
>
> **It is to live life to the fullest.**

With Jesus, life is overflowing with fun!

Jesus said, "I am come that they might have life, and that they might have it more abundantly" (John 10:10 KJV). The word *abundant* means to overflow. Jesus came to earth to teach us how to have lives that overflow with God's love!

What Does the Bible Mean when It Says My Body Is the "Temple of God"?

Through Jesus, God's Holy Spirit lives in the heart of every Christian. This means that your body is like a little temple. A *temple* is a building that welcomes and offers a home for God.

The apostle Paul asked, "Do you not know that your body is a temple of the Holy Spirit, who is in you, whom you have received from God? . . . Therefore honor God with your body" (1 Corinthians 6:19–20).

To honor God with your body means to love your body and take good care of it. Your human body is very important. God uses your body to get His work done on earth. God uses your mind to think of ways to put His love into action. God uses your feet to carry you to people who are lonely or sick or sad. God uses your arms to wrap around people who need a hug. God uses your mouth to speak kind and encouraging words. God uses your hands to gently wipe away tears.

? Why does God use your body as a temple for His Holy Spirit?

➡ **To show the world His love.**

What Does It Mean to "Put on the Armor of God"?

Life is not always easy. At some point, we all have times of sadness. We have disappointments. We have challenges. The good news is that God gives us powerful spiritual tools to help us through hard times. Over the years, these spiritual tools have become known as "putting on the armor of God."

The apostle Paul described "putting on the armor of God" like this:

Be strong in the Lord and in his mighty power. *Put on the full armor of God* . . . so that when the day of evil comes, you may be able to stand your ground, and after you have done everything, to stand. Stand firm then, with the *belt of truth* buckled around your waist, with the *breastplate of righteousness* in place, and with your *feet fitted with the readiness that comes from the gospel of peace.* In addition to all this, take up the *shield of faith*, with which you can extinguish all the flaming arrows of the evil one. Take the *helmet of salvation* and the *sword of the Spirit, which is the word of God.* And pray in the Spirit on all occasions with all kinds of prayers and requests. (Ephesians 6:10–11, 13–18; emphasis added)

How loving of God to provide us with such powerful spiritual weapons. When we put on the full armor of God, we are ready to win any battle!

What Does It Mean to Be "Salt and Light" of the World?

Jesus want us to make a positive difference in the world. Jesus wants us to love and help each other. Jesus wants us to think, talk, and act in ways that honor our Father God in heaven.

Jesus said to His disciples:

You are the salt of the earth. But if the salt loses its saltiness, how can it be made salty again? It is no longer good for anything, except to be thrown out and trampled by men. *You are the light of the world.* A city on a hill cannot be hidden. Neither do people light a lamp and put it under a bowl. Instead they put it on its stand, and it gives light to everyone in the house. In the same way, let your light shine before men, that they may see your good deeds and praise your Father in heaven. (Matthew 5:13–16; emphasis added)

What does Jesus mean when He says we are the "salt of the earth"?

Salt is a seasoning. It improves the taste of food. With the love of Jesus we can improve the world. Salt makes people thirsty. With the love of Jesus we thirst—and cause others to thirst—to know God better. Salt is used to melt ice. With the love of Jesus, our cold hearts melt with kindness and compassion. Salt is a preservative that helps food stay fresh longer. Thanks to Jesus, we live forever!

What does Jesus mean when He says we are the "light of the world"?

Light shines in the darkness. Light exposes evil and danger. Light shows people the way to safety. The love of Jesus does all these things and more. The love of Jesus shows people the way to God (John 14:6).

What Is Tithing?

Tithing is the practice of giving 10 percent of your income to God. The word *tithe* means tenth. It is first mentioned in the Old Testament, when Abraham gave "a tenth of everything" to King Melchizedek, a "priest of God Most High" (Genesis 14:17–20).

In the New Testament, we read how Jesus encouraged religious leaders to tithe (Luke 11:42). And this is what the apostle Paul wrote to the members of the early church: "On the first day of every week, each one of you should set aside a sum of money in keeping with his income" (1 Corinthians 16:2). While tithing is a good "rule of thumb" for giving, many Christians give away much *more* than 10 percent of their income!

Tithing is a way of saying thank you to God. It's a way of showing God how much you love Him. Do you get a dollar a week for allowance? You might want to give ten cents of it to God, to show that you love Him. You can give your tithe to your church. Or you can give it to another Christian organization that does good work for God. Talk to your mom and dad about this. They will have good ideas too.

In addition to giving money, there are many other ways of saying thank you to God. You can pray for other people. You can volunteer to help in a soup kitchen. You can visit a friend who is sad or lonely. You can hold a bake sale to raise money for a good Christian cause.

> Whatever you choose to **give**, God wants us to **give generously**, with a **cheerful** and **thankful** heart.
>
> (2 Corinthians 9:7)

What's the Difference Between Fasting and Dieting?

Fasting is a practice that Christians use as a way to get closer to God. To *fast* is to not eat, or eat very little, for a certain length of time. Christians often pray when they fast. We know from the Bible that Jesus expected His disciples to fast (Matthew 6:16–18). And we know that when the early Christians fasted, they also prayed (Acts 13:3).

Some Christians fast and pray when they are seeking God's guidance. Other Christians fast as a way of giving. They donate the money that they would have otherwise spent on food to a good cause. Many Christians fast during certain seasons in the church year, such as Lent. They give up something they enjoy such as chocolate or sweets as a small way of remembering how much Jesus gave up for us.

Hunger is an unpleasant feeling. Hunger caused by fasting reminds us of others who are hungry all the time. It reminds us how much we have to be thankful for. It reminds us how much we need God. Did you know that fasting occurs naturally when we sleep? The word *breakfast* means to break the fast!

Fasting and dieting are very different. Dieting is eating certain kinds and amounts of foods for the purpose of losing weight. People diet to improve their physical health. People fast to improve their spiritual health.

Most children do not fast or diet. This is because your body is still growing and you need all the good nutrition you can get. Before fasting or dieting, it is important to make sure you have your mom and dad's permission. In some cases it is important to have a doctor's permission too.

It is not necessary to fast to get closer to God. Even if you don't fast, you can always pray!

Does It Matter to God How Much Time I Spend Surfing the Net and Watching TV?

As a human being, everything you take in with your mouth, eyes, and ears affects you. Just as your mouth feeds your body, your eyes and ears feed your soul. Just as too much junk food can hurt your body, too much junk entertainment can hurt your soul.

You are a beautiful, precious child of God. You are important to God. God wants your body and soul to be healthy and strong. Some TV, movies, music, video games, and Internet sites are good. Some are not. God wants you to feed your soul with things that are wholesome, healthy, fun, and good.

The apostle Paul wrote, "Finally, brothers, whatever is true, whatever is noble, whatever is right, whatever is pure, whatever is lovely, whatever is admirable—if anything is excellent or praiseworthy—think about such things. . . . And the God of peace will be with you" (Philippians 4:8–9).

? Why does God want you to strengthen your soul with all things excellent, pure, lovely, and true?

➡ **Because God loves you.**

(1 John 3:1)

What's Wrong with Horoscopes?

God created human beings with curiosity. The word *curiosity* means the desire to know or learn. Curiosity can be very good. Curiosity leads us to explore our world. Curiosity led Christopher Columbus to America. It led astronauts to the moon. Curiosity leads us to helpful discoveries. Curiosity led Alexander Graham Bell to invent the telephone. It led Jonas Salk to invent a vaccine for polio.

But because we are human, curiosity can also have a dark side. Some people believe that occult practices such as astrology, tarot cards, and Ouija boards will give them secret knowledge about the future. The word *occult* means secret or hidden. Other occult practices include fortune telling, palm reading, numerology, witchcraft, and trying to contact the dead through people known as psychics or mediums.

God does not want us to put our faith in occult practices. God wants us to put our faith in Him. Only God knows what the future will hold. Horoscopes, tarot cards, and Ouija boards do not. Involvement with the occult leads to confusion and darkness. It does not lead to God.

In fact, God *forbids* His children to be involved with the occult. The Bible warns: "Let no one be found among you . . . who practices divination or sorcery, interprets omens, engages in witchcraft, or casts spells, or who is a medium or spiritist or who consults the dead. Anyone who does these things is detestable to the LORD" (Deuteronomy 18:10–12).

Why does God feel so strongly about the occult? Because God does not want you to be misguided or hurt. God wants you happy and well. God wants you to come to Him with your curiosity and questions. God wants to give you His good and true answers.

Why is this? Because God loves you (1 John 3:1).

Can I Have Friends Who Aren't Christians?

Yes, it is possible to be friends with people who do not know Jesus. God loves all His children. God wants us to love everyone too. At the same time, it is important to remember that because we are human, we are easily influenced by others. Good friends can be a good influence. Bad friends can be a bad influence (1 Corinthians 15:33).

Jesus had lots of different kinds of friends. Some believed in Him. Some didn't. Jesus didn't change when He was with different kinds of people. When people spoke or acted badly, He did not join in. He was always the same. He was honest and good. He was generous and kind. He was patient and forgiving. Most of all, He was loving.

As a Christian, the Bible teaches that your true home is heaven (2 Corinthians 5:1). Now here is some exciting news: being a citizen of heaven makes you an ambassador for Jesus on earth (2 Corinthians 5:20)! An *ambassador* is an official representative. Congratulations!

Being an ambassador for Jesus comes with responsibilities.

There is an old saying that "you may be the only Bible someone ever reads." This means that the words you say and the way you act can make a big impression on others—especially on friends who do not know Jesus.

How Do I Tell a Friend about Jesus?

Good news is fun to share. And knowing Jesus is good news! If you have a friend who you think might want to know more about Jesus, don't be shy. Speak right up. When the disciples worried about what to say, Jesus promised that God's Holy Spirit would give them just the right words (Mark 13:11). So relax. When it comes to telling a friend about Jesus, all you have to do is speak honestly, from your heart.

You might want to share . . .

How Jesus helps you in your day-to-day life.

How your prayers have been answered.

What you love about Jesus.

Remember that Christianity is not just another religion. Christianity is a *relationship* with the living Jesus. It's also helpful to remember that Jesus is not a legend, myth, or fairy tale. The story of Jesus does *not* begin with "Once upon a time . . ." (Luke 2:1–7). Jesus is *real*.

If your friend wants to ask Jesus into his or her heart, here is a simple prayer he or she can pray: *Jesus, I really want to know You. I believe You are the Son of God. I believe that You died for my sins. Thank You for loving me so much. Now please come into my heart and live in me. Amen.*

When your friend has prayed this prayer, encourage your friend to share this good news with his or her parents, pastor, youth minister, or other grown-up who loves Jesus. They will want to help your friend get to know Jesus better too.

What an honor it is to introduce a friend to Jesus!

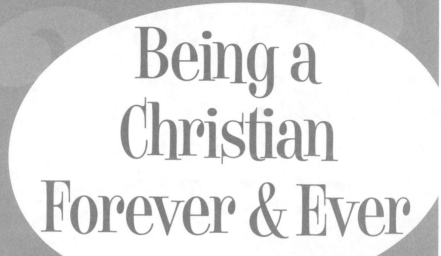

Being a Christian Forever & Ever

Why Do People Have to Die?

For human beings, death is part of the natural order of things. This is because all earthly living things, including our human bodies, are mortal. The word *mortal* means subject to death.

Death, in its way, is as natural a part of life as birth. The Bible says that for every person there is "a time to be born and a time to die" (Ecclesiastes 3:2). Still, no one wants to die. Death is sad for the people left behind. Because it is mysterious, death can be scary.

Thanks to Jesus, you don't have to be sad or scared about death. Because Jesus died for your sins and was raised from the dead, God promises that your soul can live forever in heaven (John 3:16).

Why would God promise such a wonderful thing?
Because God loves you (1 John 3:1).

What Will Happen to Me When I Die?

Death, in some ways, is a lot like birth.

Picture an unborn baby, all snug and warm in his mother's womb. For an unborn baby, the thought of being born might be pretty scary.

If the baby could talk, he might say, "What? Leave my safe, warm world that I love and know so well—a world that I've spent my *whole life* in—for someplace I know nothing about? *No way!*"

The unborn baby might be sad and scared. Maybe even angry. He might even have the mistaken idea that what was about to happen to him wasn't birth but death. After all, everything he ever knew about life was about to end.

Think how difficult it would be to explain to the unborn baby how wonderful life is on earth! How could you ever describe the brilliant colors of a rainbow? How could you begin to explain the taste of a chocolate ice-cream cone with sprinkles . . . the smell of fresh-baked cinnamon bread . . . the sound of laughter . . . the fuzzy warmth of a puppy . . . the excitement of Christmas Eve . . . the way it feels to wake up on your birthday morning?

When your body dies, your soul will begin a brand-new life in a wonderful new world called heaven. Heaven is a world that we, like an unborn baby, can barely begin to imagine (1 Corinthians 2:9).

Are There Really Angels?

Yes, there really are angels. Thousands upon thousands of them (Hebrews 12:22)! The word *angel* means messenger. The Bible says that God created the angels to be His personal messengers on earth (Hebrews 1:14).

Angels obey, worship, and praise God (Psalms 103:20; 148:2; Hebrews 1:6). Angels do not die (Luke 20:36). Angels are often described as beings of light. Because they can be so bright, angels are often pictured with golden halos around their heads (Matthew 28:3). Because they can appear and disappear so quickly, angels are often pictured with wings (Judges 6:21; Luke 1:11–12). Angels are very strong and powerful (2 Thessalonians 1:6–7; 2 Peter 2:11). They are neither male nor female. They do not marry or have baby angels (Matthew 22:30).

The Bible tells us that when angels appear to people, the first thing they often say is, "Do not be afraid!" (Judges 6:23; Luke 1:13, 30). From this, we can assume that to see one of God's angels is awesome and frightening. But God's angels refuse to be worshiped by human beings (Revelation 19:10; 22:8–9). Sometimes, if it suits God's purposes, angels can appear as human beings (Hebrews 13:2)! Maybe this is so we won't be frightened.

In the Bible two of the angels, Gabriel and Michael, are given names. God sent Gabriel to deliver important messages (Daniel 8:15; 9:21; Luke 1:19, 26). The name *Gabriel* means "God is my strength." The name *Michael* means "Who is like God?" Michael is God's archangel, or "top-level" angel, who is a warrior for God (Revelation 12:7). The Bible suggests there may be other archangels too (Daniel 10:13). In the future, when Jesus returns, He will come with many angels (Matthew 16:27).

The Bible says that God's angels are watching over us.

(Hebrews 1:14)

The Bible promises that God "will command his angels concerning you to guard you in all your ways" (Psalm 91:11).

When I Die, Will I Become an Angel with a Halo and Wings?

Human beings and angels are both created by God. But human beings and angels are two very different kinds of creatures. Human beings have mortal bodies that die and eternal souls that live forever. Angels are eternal spiritual beings. They do not have bodies that die. Angels are already living with God in heaven.

Human beings do not become angels when their bodies die. Human beings get new bodies that will never die, and join God's holy angels in heaven (1 Corinthians 15:42; 52–54; 2 Corinthians 5:1; 1 Peter 1:23 NCV).

Is It True That I Have a Guardian Angel?

Jesus said to His followers, "See that you do not look down on one of these little ones. For I tell you that their angels in heaven always see the face of my Father in heaven" (Matthew 18:10). The Bible also promises that God "will command his angels concerning you to guard you in all your ways" (Psalm 91:11).

Yes, it is true
that you have a guardian angel. Indeed, you may have **many!**

? Why does God command His angels to watch over you?

➤ Because God loves you.

(1 John 3:1)

Are There Really Demons?

Yes, there really are demons.

Human beings live in a physical world. We experience the world through our physical senses. We see, touch, hear, smell, and taste our world.

But human beings also are surrounded by an invisible, spiritual world, where God the Father, Jesus, God's Holy Spirit, and all God's holy angels live. It is also a world where demons live (Mark 1:34, 39; 6:13).

Many biblical scholars believe that demons are angels that have turned against God.

The word *demon* means evil spirit.

Angels are good. Demons are evil. Angels love God and all God's children. Demons hate God and all God's children. The leader of all the demons is Satan, who is a wicked angel. Throughout human history, God and His holy angels have been at war with Satan and his demons (Ephesians 6:12).

The good news is that thanks to Jesus, you do not need to fear Satan or his miserable demons (Romans 8:38–39). Through His death on the cross, Jesus has overcome Satan and his demons forever. Jesus has won the battle of good over evil for all time (1 Corinthians 15:57).

Is the Devil Real?

Yes, the devil is real. Today he is known as Satan.

No one knows for sure how Satan came to be. Many biblical scholars believe that he started out as one of God's archangels named Lucifer (Isaiah 14:12 KJV). The name *Lucifer* means "morning star." Lucifer was the most beautiful, brilliant, and strong of all God's creatures in heaven. But Lucifer did not want to obey God. Lucifer wanted to be worshiped like God. Lucifer wanted authority and power that did not belong to him. Lucifer's sinful jealousy toward God turned to anger and hatred.

In his anger, Lucifer rebelled and took as many as one-third of heaven's angels with him to serve as his demons. Sometimes the Bible refers to angels as "stars." When Lucifer fell, "his tail swept a third of the stars [or angels] out of the sky and flung them to the earth" (Revelation 12:4).

It is Satan who tempted Adam and Eve to sin in the Garden of Eden. It is Satan who is still busy causing trouble in the world today. In the Bible, Satan is also called a dragon, a serpent, and the devil (Revelation 12:9). The word *devil* means liar. The word *Satan* means enemy or accuser.

It is important to remember that Satan is nothing more than a furious, wicked angel. At the same time, Satan and his demons still have the power to cause much human heartache and misery. Satan is not only evil, he is very smart and tricky.

Jesus called Satan "a liar and the father of lies" (John 8:44). The apostle Paul described Satan as "the ruler of the kingdom of the air, the spirit who is now at work in those who are disobedient" (Ephesians 2:2). Paul went on to say, "For our struggle is not against flesh and blood, but against . . . the spiritual forces of evil in the heavenly realms" (Ephesians 6:12).

The apostle Peter warned, "Be self-controlled and alert. Your enemy the devil prowls around like a roaring lion looking for someone to devour" (1 Peter 5:8). The war that Satan started between good and evil continues to this day. It is being waged in heaven and on earth. It will continue until Jesus comes again with God's holy angels.

Thanks to the Bible, we know how the story ends. Happily, it is a very good and just ending!

In the end, the Bible tells us that Satan and his demons will not go unpunished. The apostle Paul wrote, "Their end will be what their actions deserve" (2 Corinthians 11:15). The apostle John wrote that after the final battle, Satan will be thrown into a lake of burning sulfur where he will be tormented day and night forever and ever (Revelation 20:10). Finally, there will be peace in heaven and on earth.

Because we know how the story ends,

in a very real sense the battle has already been won!

Because of Jesus' death on the cross for our sins and His resurrection,

Satan has already been defeated.

Even though we live with day-to-day struggles and sin,

with Jesus living in our hearts we are more than conquerors .

(Romans 8:37–39)

This is **very good** news!

Is Hell Real?

Yes, hell is real. Like heaven, hell exists outside time and space. Like heaven, sometimes there are glimpses of hell on earth. When people commit terrible acts of cruelty and murde, we get a glimpse of hell on earth. The terrible destruction and loss of human life caused by hurricanes, tornadoes, and tsunamis also give us glimpses of hell.

The word *hell* means the underworld. The Bible teaches that hell is the final dwelling place for Satan, his demons, and the souls of human beings who choose to reject God's love. The Bible describes hell as a "lake of burning sulfur" (Revelation 20:10). It is also described as a place of "eternal fire" (Matthew 25:41). These descriptions suggest that hell is an experience of unending physical pain and torment. But hell is even worse than that.

Hell is a place of eternal separation from God and His love. It is a place of unbearable emotional pain. Think how it feels when you have a really bad stomachache. It hurts a lot. But a doctor can give you medicine to make the physical pain go away. Now think how you feel when a friend talks behind your back. Or when a pet or loved one dies. The pain is much worse. There is no medicine to make emotional pain go away.

When Jesus was on the cross, He suffered for all the sins of everyone in the world. He experienced hell for us. He experienced terrible physical pain. But the emotional pain Jesus suffered was far worse.

Jesus loved God with all His heart, soul, and mind. As He was dying on the cross, the thought of being separated from God forever was almost more than Jesus could bear. He cried out, "My God, my God, why have you forsaken me?" (Matthew 27:46; Mark 15:34).

But in the end, God did not forsake Jesus. God raised Jesus from the dead! Jesus ascended to heaven to sit at the right hand of God.

Thanks to God's great love, when you die, you will not go to hell. Because God sent Jesus to die for your sins, and because you love Jesus, you will go to heaven and live forever with God and His holy angels.

Why would God do such a wonderful thing? Because God loves you. (John 3:16; 15:13; Romans 5:8; 1 John 3:1)

What Is Heaven Like?

Heaven has been in existence since before the creation of earth and human beings. Heaven exists outside time and space. Heaven is home for God the Father, Jesus, God's Holy Spirit, and God's holy angels. Heaven is also home for the souls of all human beings who know and love God. Heaven is *your* eternal home (2 Corinthians 5:1)!

Another word for heaven is paradise, which comes from a Greek word that means garden. Some people think heaven is like the Garden of Eden, before Adam and Eve were tempted by Satan to sin. The Bible also describes heaven as a spectacular eternal city known as the "new Jerusalem" (Revelation 21:2). The Bible says heaven is so bright that it "does not need the sun or the moon to shine on it, for the glory of God gives it light" (Revelation 21:23).

We know from the Bible that heaven is a wonderful place full of love, peace, forgiveness, and joy. In heaven there is no more death, sadness, crying, or pain. In heaven, God will wipe away every tear from every eye (Revelation 7:17; 21:4).

And that's just the beginning. In heaven, we will get brand-new bodies! Here on earth, our human bodies aren't designed to last forever. Over time, they get old and worn out. Or they meet with a sudden illness or accident. But our souls never die. The Bible says that in heaven our souls are wrapped in new bodies—very special bodies that will never get sick, never feel pain, and never get old. They are bodies that will live forever (1 Corinthians 15:42; 52–54; 2 Corinthians 5:1; 1 Peter 1:23 NCV)!

How all this happens is very wonderful and mysterious. "Listen," the apostle Paul wrote, "I tell you a mystery: We will not all sleep, but we will all be changed—in a flash, in the twinkling of an eye" (1 Corinthians 15:51–52).

Sometimes God gives us glimpses of heaven on earth.

Heaven is the way it feels in our hearts when we love someone. Heaven is the way it feels in our hearts when we know deep down inside that we are loved back.

How wonderful heaven will be (1 Corinthians 2:9)!

If God Loves People, Why Do Bad Things Happen?

Bad things happen. It is true. This is because the world we live in is not the way God originally created it. In the Garden of Eden, the world was in perfect harmony (Genesis 1—2). There were no hurricanes, tornadoes, or tsunamis. There were no murders, riots, or wars. There was no human pain, suffering, or death.

Because Adam and Eve chose to sin, the world and all the people in it are not the way God intended. The world and all the people in it are disordered and broken.

But God is good. We know this because the Bible says, "God is love" (1 John 4:8).

God loves the world and all the people in it. We know God loves us because He sent His only Son, Jesus, to earth to die for our sins (Romans 5:8). God did this to make a way for us to never die. God did this so that we can live with Him forever in heaven (John 3:16). That's a whole lot of love!

We also know that God is not like us. God is perfect. We are not. God sees all of human history from His throne in heaven. We can only see where we are right here and now. "'For my thoughts are not your thoughts, neither are your ways my ways,' declares the LORD. 'As the heavens are higher than the earth, so are my ways higher than your ways and my thoughts than your thoughts'" (Isaiah 55:8–9).

There are many things about God that we cannot understand. There is much about God that is a mystery or secret.

Because we trust God, we can accept His mysteries. Maybe some things are too terrible for us to know. Maybe some things are too wonderful. When God is ready, He will give us more understanding. For now, it is as though we are seeing reality through dirty glass, the Bible says. But when we get to heaven we will see everything clearly (1 Corinthians 13:12).

In the Bible, God promises that one day there will be a new heaven and a new earth (Revelation 21:1). The battle between good and evil being waged in heaven and on earth will end. Good will triumph over evil.

Until that day, bad things will happen. It's part of life and being human. But here is good news: because God loves us, He promises to help us through the bad times.

How can we know this is true?
Because God always keeps His promises (Deuteronomy 7:9; 1 Corinthians 1:9).

Why Do People Hurt Other People?

People are not perfect. People hurt other people for many reasons. Sometimes they are afraid. Sometimes they are sick. Sometimes they are sad. Sometimes people hurt others because they have been hurt themselves.

When I was a little girl, I had a beautiful fawn boxer named Roxie. Roxie the boxer belonged to another family before she came to our home. The other family used to go away on long trips. When they did, they locked Roxie in their cold, dark basement. Roxie didn't like that. She panicked and barked and scratched at the basement door. Sometimes she scratched the door so hard that her paws bled.

Shortly after Roxie came to live with us, we had to go away on a trip. The minute Roxie saw my open suitcase, she looked at me with panicky eyes and ran away! It took my dad an hour to catch her. I loved Roxie. It hurt my feelings that Roxie would run away. But then my dad explained to me that Roxie acted that way because she was afraid. Roxie acted that way because she had been hurt by her other owner. Roxie didn't want to be hurt again.

Now I have a roly-poly pug named Max. I got Max when he was a fluffy little puppy, just ten weeks old.

Max has only known human kindness, and he is the happiest, roly-poliest pug I know. When he sees an open suitcase, he jumps in, rolls on his back, and waits for me to tickle his tummy.

> **People hurt one another, it is true.**
> **People are not perfect. But we can always try to show each other human love and kindness.**
> (John 13:34–35)
>
> **And we can always pray for one another.**
> (Romans 12:12; 1 Thessalonians 5:17).

How Can Anything Good Come out of Pain and Suffering?

Everyone experiences pain and suffering in life. It is part of being human. Like death, suffering is something that all human beings have in common. We know it must be important, because God Himself experienced pain and suffering on the cross.

God does not cause pain and suffering. But God can take pain and suffering and turn it into something beautiful and good.

We see this in nature. Think of a pearl. A pearl starts as a bit of sand that gets trapped in an oyster. The sand scratches and irritates the oyster. The oyster reacts by covering the grain of sand with layer upon layer of a smooth protective coating. Over time, the nasty bit of sand becomes a beautiful pearl! Sometimes we can have a difficult person in our life. But when we cover the person with layer upon layer of love and prayers, we find that the person no longer irritates or troubles us. In fact, the person may become a beautiful friend!

God is able to create something beautiful from even the most terrible kind of pain and suffering. I have a friend whose father died suddenly. The fact that her father died was a terrible thing. My friend cried and cried. How could anything good come out of something so sad?

Years later, my own dad died. During that sad time, my friend was the one person who understood the pain I was going through. Out of the terrible sadness of losing her father, my friend had gained the beautiful gift of compassion. The word *compassion* means to suffer with. My friend's compassion was like a little bit of heaven falling into my world of loss and sadness.

The best example of God turning evil into good is when He resurrected Jesus from the dead. Because Jesus rose from the dead, so, too, will everyone who believes in Him!

When we experience pain and suffering, we can be comforted by God's promises in the Bible. When Joseph was treated badly by his brothers, he forgave them, saying, "You intended to harm me, but *God intended it for good* to accomplish what is now being done, the saving of many lives" (Genesis 50:20; emphasis added). The apostle Paul wrote, "And we know that in all things *God works for the good* of those who love him, who have been called according to his purpose" (Romans 8:28; emphasis added).

God can take anything and turn it into something good.
Even pain and suffering.

Do People Who Never Heard of Jesus Go to Heaven Too?

Throughout human history, not everyone has had the chance to hear the good news about Jesus. Many people lived and died before Jesus was born. Even today, there are millions of people who have yet to hear about Jesus.

The Bible says that God is everywhere. Even when people have never heard about God, they can know God as their Creator through the mystery and beauty of nature, and through the miracle of life (Psalm 19). But the only way people can get to know God as their personal loving Daddy, or "Abba" *Father* is through knowing His Son, Jesus (John 14:6). Knowing Jesus is God's way for people to understand and experience His great forgiveness and love (John 3:16; 14:7).

We know from the Bible that God is perfect in every way. God is loving. God is patient. God is wise. God is forgiving. God is fair. God is good. God is all-knowing. God knows the heart of every human being. Because God is perfect, we can trust that He will make the right choice about who does or doesn't go to heaven. And that includes people who have never heard of Jesus.

Who does or doesn't go to heaven is something God does not want you to worry about. It is, however, something He does want you to *do* something about!

What does God want you to do?

1. God wants you to love Him (Deuteronomy 6:4–5; Matthew 22:35–37).
2. God wants you to love others (John 13:34; Romans 12:10).
3. God wants you to try your best, with Jesus living in your heart, to live a life that is pleasing to God (Romans 12:1).
4. God wants you to read your Bible (2 Timothy 3:15–16).
5. God wants you to share with others the good news about Jesus (Matthew 28:18–20; Mark 16:15).
6. God wants you to pray for the world and all the people in it (Romans 12:12; 1 Thessalonians 5:17)

What will happen when you do these things?

When you meet God in heaven, He will wrap His big, strong arms around you and say, "Well done, my good and faithful servant! Come and share my joy!" (see Matthew 25:23).

Can I Believe in Science and Still Believe in God?

Yes, you can believe in science and still believe in God.

It is helpful to remember that the Bible was not written by modern-day scientists.

The Bible was written thousands of years ago by men of faith. In fact, when the Bible was written, science as we know it didn't even exist! When the Bible was written, people didn't know that our planet earth is like a beautiful blue marble, spinning in the darkness of space. People didn't know that an invisible force called gravity is what causes objects to fall to the ground. People didn't know that diseases are caused by tiny, squiggly germs and viruses that can only be seen with a microscope. In fact, the microscope would not be invented for thousands of years!

God created the universe. Science is the ongoing effort of human beings to understand how God's creation works.

Dr. Francis S. Collins, M.D., Ph.D., is the Director of the National Human Genome Research Institute at the National Institutes of Health. Dr. Collins is a brilliant scientist. He is also a man of faith who loves Jesus. He says, "I see no conflict in what the Bible tells me about God and what science tells me about nature."

I have a friend who is a sixth-grade science teacher. She is also a person of faith who loves Jesus. "When I look at a rainbow," she says, "science tells me that I am looking at white light hitting water droplets suspended in the air. Science tells me that the rainbow is caused by the light breaking up into a spectrum of seven colors. But being a person of faith, I can also say, 'Thank You, God, for creating such a beautiful rainbow!' I remember the story of Noah's ark and appreciate the rainbow as a symbol of God's love" (Genesis 9:16).

> **Science can tell you what life is made of. But science cannot tell you what life is for. Only God, who loves you, can do that.**

Does God Still Love People Who Choose Not to Believe in Him?

Yes, God loves all people, whether they believe in Him or not. This is because God is a loving Father (Matthew 5:45). There is no place a person can go and no thought a person can think that will make God stop loving him. At the same time, when a person chooses not to believe in Him, it makes God *very* sad.

But God never gives up. Because He is a loving Father, God waits patiently for His children to return to Him. Day and night, He scans the horizon (Luke 15:11–32).

Day and night, He calls each of His children by name. How happy God is when a lost child hears His voice! How happy God is when a lost child returns! The Bible says that angels sing and all heaven rejoices (Luke 15:10).

Here is good news:

It is never too late to come home to God. You can be ten years old or one hundred years old. God is always waiting with open arms for His children to come to Him.

? Why does God wait so patiently for His children?
➡ Because God is **love.**
(1 John 4:8)

The Most Important Prayer in the World

Maybe you've been going to church since you were a little kid. Maybe you've read this whole book cover to cover. Maybe you've done all these things, but you're still *not sure* that Jesus is living in your heart. Not to worry! We all feel that way sometimes.

Jesus says, "Here I am! I stand at the door and knock. If anyone hears my voice and opens the door, I will come in" (Revelation 3:20).

Do you hear Jesus **knocking** on the **door** of your heart? If you do, maybe **now** is the time for you to open the door. It's easy. Just say:

Thank You, Jesus, for being real. Thank You for loving me so much that You died on the cross for me and my sins. It's hard to believe that You love me that much. But I do. Thank You, Jesus, for forgiving me when I sin. Thank You for loving me no matter what. Please come into my heart now, live in me, and be my friend forever. Day by day, show me what You want me to do. Help me hear Your voice. Help me be obedient. Help me read my Bible. Lead me to good Christian friends. Teach me to love. Thank You, Jesus, for hearing this prayer. In Your name, I pray, amen.

Now that you've prayed this prayer, you may not *feel* any different, but deep down inside you *are*. Get ready for some real fun and excitement, because you are about to embark on a new adventure!

From this moment on, wherever you go, whatever you do, Jesus *promises* that He will be with you. Jesus *promises* that He will be living in your heart, helping and loving you. Whenever you want Jesus, just call His name. He will be with you, listening, caring, and protecting you. Jesus will be the best friend you ever had (John 15:15).

> Now that you've invited Jesus into your heart, tell your parents or another trusted grown-up who loves Jesus. They will want to celebrate with you! Ask them what it means to love God. Ask them what it means to be baptized and to follow Jesus. They will want to help you take the first steps in your journey of faith.

? Why does Jesus want to do all this for you?

➡ **Because Jesus loves you.**
(John 15:9, 13; 1 John 3:16)

Make your own
"God's Promises for You"
Promise Teller!

A paper promise teller is a fun way to keep God's promises at your fingertips . . . and share God's promises with your friends!

HERE IS HOW TO MAKE YOUR OWN
"God's Promises for You" Promise Teller:

Cut pattern on dotted line (on page 223) and remove from book. Use a copier to print copies of the pattern for however many promise keepers you want to make.

Fold a corner into the central point.

Repeat with the opposite corner.

Repeat with the other two corners.

You'll end up with a square.

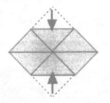 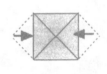

Flip the paper over.

Fold a corner over to the center.

Repeat with the opposite corner.

Fold over the two remaining corners.

You'll end up with a smaller square.

Fold the square in half.

Unfold and fold in half the other way.

Unfold and pull the four ends together, making a diamond-like shape.

Pick up each of the four square flaps, and insert your thumbs

and index fingers of both hands inside the four pockets.

You will be able to move the four parts around.

"God's Promises for You"
Promise Teller

Cut here and fold to make your own "God's Promises for You" Promise Teller!